Praise for *Let the Mo*

"Foreman, an undaunted truth-seeker, describes herself as 'a regular old human being . . . trying to understand what we are all doing here.' If this is true, the rest of us ordinary humans can take heart. She is the perfect example of what William Faulkner said, stressing his belief that humanity 'will not merely endure: (we) will prevail.' She has given us a testament to the resilience of a spirit ever reaching toward love. And finding it.

—MARA WAGNER, psychoanalyst and professor at the Boston Graduate School of Psychoanalysis

"Foreman's lovely memoir about growing up with abusive and emotionally absent parents is transformative and shiningly hopeful. The book delivers funny and wise vignettes sometimes set in the vibrant newsroom of *The Boston Globe*, where she worked as a journalist for decades. Foreman exudes a courageous determination to discover how to give and receive life-changing love despite a childhood where love was nowhere to be found. From where I sit as a therapist who works with trauma survivors, this is nothing short of a miracle. A wonderful, wonderful read."

—EILEEN LYNCH, psychologist specializing in complex trauma

"Wonderful! I laughed, feared, and cried throughout this talented woman's courageous sharing of the truths, loving, traumas, and impermanence of our lives. As a syndicated medical journalist, musician, and woman who dares to look inward, Judy Foreman has embraced the opposite of her childhood silence. The reader is healed and informed."

—JOHN LIVINGSTONE, MD, former Director in Child and Adolescent Psychiatry and Consultant in Clinician Selfcare, Harvard Medical School

Let the
More
Loving
One
Be Me

Let the More Loving One Be Me

MY JOURNEY FROM TRAUMA TO FREEDOM

Judy Foreman

SHE WRITES PRESS

Published 2023
Printed in the United States of America

Print ISBN: 978-1-64742-596-8
E-ISBN: 978-1-64742-597-5
Library of Congress Control Number: 2023904759

For information, address:
She Writes Press
1569 Solano Ave #546
Berkeley, CA 94707

She Writes Press is a division of SparkPoint Studio, LLC.

All company and/or product names may be trade names, logos, trademarks, and/or registered trademarks and are the property of their respective owners.

Names and identifying characteristics have been changed to protect the privacy of certain individuals.

Interior design and typeset by Katherine Lloyd, The DESK

The following articles are reprinted with permission from *The Boston Globe.*
"A Healing Hope—Lessons from the Lodz Ghetto," © Aug. 10, 2009.
"Poetic Justice in the First Round,"© Mar. 20, 1982
"Watching Nora Die," ©June 30, 1996.
"They said I might have breast cancer. Why would I need to wait weeks for a biopsy?" © Mar. 32, 2022.

"Material Wealth Means…" © Dec. 3, 1973, reprinted with permission from *The Lowell Sun.*

To my precious husband, Ken.
You're my everything.

CHAPTER ONE

Danger

He never touched me.

Still, it was decades before I could tell my mother about it, a feat I managed only when it was clear that she was dying. My mother seemed shocked at this belated telling, but how could she have been? Where did she think her husband was disappearing to, half naked, every night?

I remember his penis, much as I would rather not. It terrified and disgusted me. He would come to my bedroom door, open it, and stand in the doorway, clad only in a T-shirt, his potbelly sagging and hairy, the hairs sticking out from under the shirt hem.

Above the neck of his T-shirt, his face erupted, oversized, two chins sinking down to touch the edge of his shirt, the dim light from the hallway bouncing off his hairless head, his thick, bushy eyebrows—the hairs poked up every which way—casting his eyes into shadow. His penis just hung there between his legs—pink, fleshy, an appendage, menacing, almost alive. This image, unerasable, set me up for a lifetime of insomnia, a fear of falling asleep. I couldn't afford to go to sleep. I didn't want to be surprised.

Bad things were not supposed to happen in a house like this.

This was Westchester County, an upper-middle-class neighborhood outside New York City. A chandelier, bought on one of my parents' many European trips, hung ostentatiously in the hallway, its delicate components having been assembled by workmen hired particularly for this task, its job not so much to shed light in the hallway but to make clear to all who entered that this was a house of success, the house of a self-made man. This was a house of Waterford crystal and Evesham china, not the plastic tablecloths and mismatched plates and glasses of the house in the Pennsylvania coal-mining town where my father grew up, a house he was always ashamed of.

The suburban house had all the ornaments a big corporate executive needed—expensive suits and silk ascots from Harrods hanging in his closet above the rows of soft leather shoes, an ever-smiling wife always at home with dinner waiting, and the other two props such an important man needed to complete the picture: my younger brother and me. We were ornaments, my brother and I, living proof of the corporate man's success.

And so it went, every night until I finally went to college. Every night, I would hear his footsteps coming down the hall, getting closer and closer with each breath I took. Hastily, I would switch off my light, hoping I had been fast enough that no light would show under the door-sill when he turned the corner toward my room. I would burrow down, squeezing my eyes shut, feigning sleep the way a small, frightened animal plays dead. I got hot huddled under the blankets, yet my body was stiff, frozen in fear.

In the beginning, I was too young to know the word "rape"—after all, I was only twelve when the nightly exposure started—but my brain knew somehow, knew deep down that this, whatever it was called, was wrong, horribly wrong, that fathers were not supposed to stand there in the semidarkness exposing themselves to their daughters.

What if he came all the way into my room? What if he could tell I was awake? What if it didn't matter whether I was awake or not? What if he lay down on top of me, his heavy, awkward body squashing me? Would I be able to breathe? What if he took the covers off? What if ... ?

He always smelled terrible, reeking of stale man-sweat. By this time of night, his breath would be sour, too. At dinner, he would keep the full crystal decanter close by his wineglass, all the wine for him.

Danger

He barely glanced at the rest of us, my mother at one end of the table, facing him, smiling the way the women's magazines said to, my brother slouched miserably, directly across the table from me.

After the wine had worked its dark magic, he would start to cry. Nobody ever knew why. Nobody looked at him. Nobody knew what to do except wait for dinner to be over.

"I love this family so much," he would sob, his chest heaving, fat tears rolling down his cheeks. "Families are everything. This is a happy family," he would say as my mother, nervous, looked on encouragingly.

Everybody stared at their plates.

"Look at me," he would jerk up and snarl to my brother, who would slide down in his chair, his food untouched.

"Stop," my mother would protest feebly. "Stop."

"You stop."

My brother would cry. In our father's eyes, my brother couldn't do anything right, especially sports. But that was partly because he couldn't see out of his left eye. And that was because he no longer had a left eye. Because of my father. That is another story.

There was so much I didn't understand, then or for years afterward. A child only knows the world she is born into. Her parents are all there is, her only reality. That world is supposed to be a safe haven. But mine wasn't.

At night, as always, my father would knock on my door. "Are you awake?"

I would pretend not to hear.

"I just wanted to say good night."

I would say nothing.

"Are you sure you are not awake?" he would persist.

"I was just falling asleep," I would mumble, afraid to not respond at all.

"I just wanted to talk," he would say, then silently walk away.

Nothing actually happened. So why did I feel raped?

After all, he never touched me.

ॐ

I am content. Happy, even.

This was not a foregone conclusion. In fact, it was pretty unlikely, given the family I grew up in.

I grew up in danger. In danger because of a sexually abusive, alcoholic, and rageful father. And in danger because of a mother who was terrified of feelings—her angry husband's, certainly; her own, presumably; and mine, because of how utterly family destroying it would have been to have a little child speak the truth of how terrifying the family really was.

My father was a large man, and not just physically. He was a vice president of one of America's largest corporations, a larger-than-life figure to most adults and certainly to me as a young child.

He was physically imposing, a good six feet, massive, though neither obese nor muscular. He had enormous, straggly eyebrows and a large bald head. His voice was stentorian. In adulthood, he sang bass, loudly, in the church choir. In college, he dabbled in stage acting. I have little doubt that his voice could carry to the farthest balcony; it certainly dominated the dining room table.

My father was not a handsome man. It was difficult to look at his face because his eyes were cold and small compared to the rest of him. His body radiated tension with every gesture, every word. An irritable, anxious man, he was a caged tiger, ready to pounce. My being slow to bring him after-dinner tea would trigger a growl. My brother slumping in his chair would occasion a sharp reprimand. Even scrambled eggs drew his ire if they didn't clump up on time.

A Trumpian figure, he was narcissistic and authoritarian, easily wounded, physically awkward, chronically angry. He cried as easily as he raged, especially after his wine at dinner, and I could never figure out how to handle either the tears or the rage. To a psychiatrist, he would have been called a "depressed alcoholic." To us, he was simply "terrifying."

He was the only important one in the family. The rest of us tiptoed around him. No one else's feelings or needs mattered or could even be spoken aloud. At his insistence, we had regular, dreadful "family meetings," where he was the only one who could speak with impunity. He ran these tense sessions like the corporate executive he was, never seeming to get the difference between work and family.

My brother and I were not allowed to call him "Dad." We knew he was our real father, not some stepfather, but we had to address him by his first name. He mocked me when, as a teenager, I begged to call him "Dad."

"So what should I call you?" he taunted. "Daughter?"

No one dared cross him, lest his rage, just millimeters beneath the surface, be triggered. Early in adolescence, I developed the habit of twisting my hair with my left hand at the dinner table so I would not have to look at him. To avoid him after dinner, I spent hours alone studying in my bedroom. Summers, I'd sit alone outside in the backyard with the little statues of the characters from a board game, moving them around in pretend scenarios of happy families.

He never actually hit any of us—my mother, my brother, or me—unless you count spankings with what we called the "fish paddle," a small wooden paddle that he used to cut up fish food for the angel fish in his aquarium. But on the eve of my first wedding, he did tell Bruce, my soon-to-be first husband, that if I ever got out of line, to go ahead and smack me. That advice, thankfully, was totally ignored.

My father grew up in a small, gritty town in western Pennsylvania, a town he hated visiting, for reasons I never fully understood. He was secretive about his growing up. I know only a few of his childhood stories: That his mother once made him drown a litter of kittens. That he was sick a lot as a child and spent long weeks in bed reading. That his younger brother died of polio. That his father, who ran a dry-cleaning shop, went under financially and emotionally during the Depression and never recovered from either.

That tragedy left a lasting impression on my father, creating a desperation not to "fail," as he thought his own father had, but to get rich. Which he did until, against my mother's better judgment, he invested heavily in a risky real estate company and went bankrupt. At one point he was in debt to thirteen banks. Money was the ever-elusive goal, but despite his millions, it was never enough. He was a rich man but an empty one.

He never admitted he was an alcoholic and never attended AA. He made it a point never to have three-martini lunches at work, as he said other businessmen did, but saved his drinking for home, for us. He would buy wine by the box with a little spout for easy refills. The alcohol never seemed to make him jolly, just sadder and angrier. He and my mother would say only that he had an "allergy" to alcohol. Eventually, he quit drinking, but sobriety did little to change his underlying personality.

Even when sober, he would make frequent inappropriate sexual comments to adult women guests, urging them to take off their clothes and go skinny-dipping with him in the pond by our house. My mother would try to hush him and guide the startled women to the kitchen. Preoccupied by sex, he would shame me at dinner when I had period cramps, asking what was wrong with my ovaries. After one trip to Australia with my mother, when I asked what he liked best, he said, "The tits, the tits." Incredibly, he actually dropped his pants when my brother brought his new fiancée to dinner. He even said once that he wanted my brother and me, still young, to watch him having sex with our mother. Mercifully, that never happened.

But the sexual abuse did, night after night when I was a teenager. I told no one.

Danger

Only later in life did a series of "mini strokes" slightly dent his domineering nature, making him a bit softer. Only then, for the first time I can remember, did he tell me I was pretty. Only then did he seem to like me. Eventually, he became dependent on my mother, though still unable to accept vulnerability. When he finally needed a cane, he refused to use one, insisting that my mother, despite her bad knees and leukemia, be his cane.

And then there was my mother.

It was my mother who encouraged me to travel, to go on a youth cycling trip one summer, to become an American Field Service student living with a Danish family for another summer, to spend yet another summer traveling all through Europe with my college roommate.

My mother was the one who encouraged me to play the clarinet and join the band. To open a bank account and learn to write checks. She taught me to canoe smoothly and quietly. She taught me to swim around the dock at the house of some friends and, eventually, all the way across the lake, with her paddling beside me, a youthful feat that instilled in me a lifelong love of the water and of swimming. She taught me to decipher foreign phrases, to love foreign languages to the point that, for a while, I seriously considered becoming a professional linguist. A devoted stargazer, she taught me to recognize the constellations. And how to garden. I learned from her how to lay out a garden so it didn't look too rigid or box-like. How to pick the right plants for shade, and for sun. To plant things so that *something* was flowering all summer. And most of all, to enjoy the feel of the earth, the scent of the flowers, the peace of a sunset moment in nature.

Until she married my father, my mother was apparently a spunky person. She was the son her father always wanted. They rode horses together. They sailed together, and she taught us to call him by his nautical nickname, "Skipper." In high school, she played drums and the French horn.

Though she remained pretty and charming, most of my mother's playful spirit disappeared when she became a submissive wife. (My parents met at a party where my father was lecturing the partygoers on swimming by lying on his stomach on a hassock, demonstrating the crawl. Only later did my mother learn he could not swim a stroke.)

I think that, in some ways, despite my father's domineering personality, my mother truly loved being the wife of an important man, and, given that her own parents were not wealthy, I am sure she loved the money, too.

She saw herself as the quintessential corporate wife. And that, of course, was what I was supposed to be, too. Once, when my then-fiancé, Bruce, and I were staying at my parents' house for the summer, I was getting ready to accompany him as he drove around visiting customers for his job as an insurance salesman. He was all dressed up. I wore jeans and a shirt, intending to sit and read in the car while he made his house calls.

My mother took one look at me and gasped. "You can't go like that. You have to learn to be a good corporate wife." I argued that no one would see me just sitting in the car; then, as usual for my still-intimidated self, I caved and promptly changed my clothes.

For all the harm my father did, the damage from my mother was, in some ways, worse. She was an enigma, physically present but emotionally absent, there but not there. This was intensely confusing for me. If I felt sad, she would deny those feelings, suggesting instead that I must have a cold or a stomach ache. Instead of consoling me or asking me why I felt that way, she assumed something was wrong with me; not surprisingly, my child-self took that message to heart, internalizing the belief that there was something intrinsically bad and wrong about sadness. She herself, ever chipper, never admitted to sadness or any other deep feeling. If she had, she might have left him, a radical act in those days.

Danger

I can't remember her ever snuggling me or consoling me or reassuring me. Decades later, when I was getting over my second husband's death, a dear friend said, "Everything is going to be all right." With a shock, I realized I couldn't recall my mother ever saying those words to me, giving me that reassurance, or even holding me.

Indeed, my deepest feelings as a child were of profound emptiness, of no one being there, the sheer infant terror of being left alone, invisible. Nobody home. My father was frightening. But it was my mother's emotional not-there-ness that left me for a long time without a center, and with deep feelings of abandonment.

And so, I looked to the outside world. School. What else could I do? To a child like me whose home was not safe, school felt like salvation, sanity. A child has to find something to attach to, and if it's not a parent, it has to be something, or somebody, else.

My grandparents helped a little. With my grandmother, Baba, and "Skipper," I was not invisible. I was special. When I had dinner at their house, Baba would cook lamb chops for me. She let me eat dessert first. She made a fuss about me. Even as a small child, when she would come over to visit, I would sneak outside and hide in her car, on the floor behind the driver's seat. I hoped she wouldn't see me there until she got home, so I could stay with her. But usually, she caught on to my trick and made me go home to my mother.

I learned much later, as a young *Boston Globe* reporter covering a conference on alcoholic and abusive families, that my family fit a typical alcoholic, abusive pattern. A conference speaker was describing such families as having tight boundaries *around* the family but loose boundaries *within* it. I was stunned. This was us. Only then did I recall that my father had explicitly and repeatedly forbidden us to talk about the family to anyone outside the four of us—a nondisclosure agreement without the handshake or the money. Such secrets are the hallmarks of unsafe families.

And there are so, so many unsafe families.

I have a friend whose brother sexually abused her every night, then warned, "Don't tell." For years, she didn't. When she finally did, her family fell apart. I have a friend who was raped by her live-in grandfather. She told no one for years.

I have another friend whose stepfather, a former priest, shoved her headfirst into a snowbank when she was six, nearly suffocating her. He then raped her when she was eleven.

I have a friend who was first raped by her father, an MD and a university professor, when she was three. She is still grappling with it. Her sister committed suicide.

These are women whom I happen to know well. I did not seek them out to make a point. Only over time did I learn their stories, and stories from other women friends too.

By comparison, my father's nightly exposure of himself to me, a kind of psychological rape, may seem mild, but it wasn't. I never knew when it might be physical rape.

Sexual violence, defined as sexual activity in which consent is not obtained or freely given, is widespread, affecting millions of people, most of them female, every year, according to the Centers for Disease Control and Prevention. Put starkly, an American is sexually assaulted every seventy-three seconds, according to the Rape, Abuse & Incest National Network, with most victims under thirty years of age; a child is victimized every nine minutes.

CDC figures show that nearly one in five American women (more than 18 percent) experiences completed or attempted rape during her lifetime. For males, other data show the figure is 1.4 percent. But these figures, striking as they are, are almost certainly underestimates because, as a team of Virginia researchers pointed out in a 2005 paper, most sexual assaults are not reported to authorities.

The Virginia researchers conducted a randomized telephone

survey of nearly two thousand women aged eighteen or older. The prevalence of sexual assault was 27.6 percent, and most of these assaults were rapes. A whopping 78 percent of the victims reported that the sexual assault occurred for the first time *when they were children or adolescents.*

Other data show that one in three female rape victims experienced rape for the first time between eleven and seventeen years of age. And one in eight female rape victims reported that it occurred before age ten.

Perhaps most disturbing, more than 90 percent of child sexual abuse victims know their attackers. In fact, the majority (77.5 percent) of perpetrators were *parents* of the victim, according to US Department of Justice figures.

So, how did I escape?

This book is that story, the story of my slow liberation, my gradual disentangling from my dangerous family. It is, ultimately, a story of the freeing of a soul.

It is the story of a young woman who stumbled into the tremendous gift of a gratifying career—journalism, an enterprise that centers on the very thing I never had as a child: the ability, indeed the permission, the necessity, of speaking the truth right out loud.

It is the story of a personal search for meaning and healing through meditation, psychotherapy, and plain old self-reflection. This search isn't over and probably never will be. It is the search for the kindness and self-compassion to recognize and befriend the traumatized parts of my soul, though getting to the truth of my family, the root of my character, has taken decades.

And it is the story of love and marriage—or, to be precise, three marriages—each man remarkably appropriate for the stage of life I was in and the amount of intimacy I could tolerate. The first was passionate, adventurous, and immature; the second, peaceful, stable, and lovely; the third, once again passionate, but this time far more intimate, occasionally tumultuous, but ultimately it was the deepest connection of two souls.

I have been lucky enough, in other words, to have the two things that Freud (and I) believe matter most in life, though he put it better than I: "Love and work are the cornerstones of our humanness." I have had to work hard for both. It has been well worth it.

CHAPTER TWO

ᏉNobody Home

G rowing up with an alcoholic parent is a lonely, frightening business.

Even when there's another (nonalcoholic) parent around, that parent may be so busy placating the alcoholic and denying the problem that *that* parent isn't really there either. The family is empty.

This translates into a childhood marked by some degree of abuse, neglect, or both. And an adulthood marked by trying to "re-parent" oneself, to give oneself the emotional security that should have been there all along.

I should know.

I am one of the millions of American adults—one in every five, according to the American Academy of Child and Adolescent Psychiatry—who grew up in an alcoholic home. Some put the figure at one in four. Violence is often part of the pattern, though thankfully, not in my case. One of every eight kids who grow up in alcoholic homes witnesses their mother being beaten or hit, according to a leading medical journal.

While it's widely known how deadly alcohol abuse can be to the drinker—alcohol kills 95,000 Americans a year, making it the third leading cause of preventable death after tobacco and poor diet/physical inactivity—what's less widely recognized, at least among laypeople, is the extent of emotional harm suffered by growing up in an alcoholic family.

But sociologists, psychotherapists, and medical professionals do know what happens to a child's mind in an alcoholic family. And it's not pretty. Trust and security, for instance, are nowhere to be found in an alcoholic home. The very people who are supposed to be grown-ups, sources of comfort and safety, simply aren't.

Instead of security, there is only danger and uncertainty. In a child's still-forming mind, this creates the unconscious belief that the world *at large*, not just the home, cannot be trusted and that no place, even within one's own mind, is truly safe.

In other words, the rules of growing up in an alcoholic family become: "Don't talk. Don't trust. Don't feel," as Father Joseph Martin, a priest, recovering alcoholic, and renowned speaker on addiction puts it.

The surprising thing, as social psychologist Claudia Black notes in her best-selling book *It Will Never Happen to Me*, is that many children growing up in alcoholic homes never come to the attention of school counselors, ministers, or other outsiders. They slip under the radar, too well-behaved to cause trouble, get bad grades, or wind up in doctors' offices with vague somatic complaints.

Some children in alcoholic families become so "good," so overly responsible, that when their father or mother starts drinking, they grab coats and pajamas and take their siblings to the neighbors' house for safety. These kids learn early that they can't rely on others, so they rely only on themselves. This works for a while, but as they grow older, adult children of alcoholics can experience a loneliness that simply doesn't make sense to them.

I can attest to that. My father was not a falling-down drunk. He never lost his job. As I've said, he was a high-powered businessman. Our house was neat and clean. My mother looked pretty and gave nice parties. We were never poor. But tension and denial ruled the day. All feelings had to be stuffed, denied.

This makes sense now, though it didn't at the time. For my mother to be able to hear my feelings, she would have had to acknowledge her own. And her own had to have been anger, disappointment, and eventually the realization that she would have to leave this tyrannical man. And where would that have gotten her? With no career, two years of college, and no money of her own, what were her options? I'm sure she saw none.

In an alcoholic family like mine, the whole idea of normal life just doesn't exist. If you don't grow up experiencing what normal is, you end up guessing what it must be. And spending years learning to tell truth from lies. My father's rages were hushed up by my mother insisting, "He really is a wonderful man. We have a wonderful marriage. We wake up holding hands."

It took me years to know deeply how much of a lie those statements were. And to even realize that this alcoholic family of mine was not normal, that this was not how most kids grew up, that not everybody goes home to a rageful father and a mother determined to deny it all.

༉

There we stood, maybe thirty of us in our matching blue T-shirts emblazoned with "Duzzins of Cuzzins" on the front and "Foreman Family Reunion" on the back. A family we were not. So few of us even knew each other that we had to wear name tags on our T-shirts.

My father, now in his seventies, had despised his parents, barely seeing them since leaving home as a young man. A hugely successful businessman with a broken soul, he had suddenly, desperately needed to concoct a family out of the shreds of people he had forsaken decades earlier.

On his orders, my mother and his sister began organizing this so-called reunion. My father's sister had stayed behind in the dreary Pennsylvania town where they grew up in order to care for their parents, while he moved east to make his fortune. The two women called or wrote to all the relatives they could unearth, no matter how genetically or physically distant. All were invited to the showplace, the house in Connecticut that my father had built, a monument to corporate America and to his ego.

I had dreaded the event for weeks. I had my second husband, Tom, and my teenage son with me, too. Added protection. The first day of the reunion was blissfully uneventful, and it was already Saturday noon. Only twenty-four hours to go.

The thirty of us lined up, more or less by height and age, on the back deck. Cross, as usual, and perspiring heavily, my father fiddled with his camera, looking up often to snap at hapless relatives who strayed from their assigned positions or tried to change places with each other. He swore at the dogs that darted in and out. He bellowed for my mother, who was still in the kitchen frantically organizing final lunch buffet details.

"Smile, everyone," my father commanded, his own face a sweaty rictus of impatience.

I couldn't. How could I smile—on command, no less—at this man?

"Smile, goddammit!" he snarled at me. I burst into tears and ran off the deck, gesturing urgently for Tom and my son to come with me. "I'm leaving! We're going home!" I screamed.

I ran upstairs to pack, my guys rushing after me.

"You did the right thing," said Tom gently, snatching his shirts off hangers.

"It's okay, Mom," added my son, tucking his skateboard under his arm. "I didn't want to stay anyway."

As the three of us threw clothes and books into bags, my father stormed violently into the room, my mother close on his heels.

"I am cutting you out of the will!" he yelled, enraged.

"No," my mother protested weakly. "Don't. Please."

I found a short burst of courage and turned to face him: "I always knew money was the secret string you controlled me with. I'm glad you finally said it out loud." I grabbed Tom's hand. "Let's go."

In shocked silence, my parents watched us gather our bags and head downstairs. They followed.

As Tom and my son put the bags in the car, I stood, still shaking, in the hallway, facing my father. My mother put her arm around my waist. A few of the stunned cousins peeked around the corner, then scuttled away.

"You wonder why I never come here." I looked my father hard in the eye. "It's because you're always so angry. I thought it would get better when you stopped drinking, but it hasn't."

"Listen to her," said my mother, half hiding behind me. "She's telling the truth."

I'm fighting her battles too, I thought with a jolt. Maybe she's on my side now. Finally. I drove home in tears.

My mother didn't call for three weeks.

I don't know exactly when my father started drinking or why, but the pattern of an angry, bullying father and an emotionally absent mother is not uncommon.

But while some kids growing up in a family like this band together for safety and companionship, my brother and I did not. In fact, one of the saddest things for me about growing up in the family I did is that my parents practiced a kind of "divide and conquer" strategy toward my brother and me. Thinking back on it now, I was a kind of orphan. My brother was, too. In a way, all four of us probably were, each in his or her lonely silo.

My brother and I never talked with each other about our parents. I believe my father forbade it, and we obviously would never have crossed him. And my mother wouldn't tolerate it. To speak of my father's drinking and authoritarian behavior would have punctured her denial of the happy, suburban family she wanted us to be.

As kids, my brother and I had separate rooms starting when I was about eleven and my brother, eight. We never knocked on each other's door or whispered in the hall or took walks together. I had some friends, but my brother pretty much stayed in his room except for TV and dinner. He seemed withdrawn, had trouble in school, and didn't take good care of himself—he never brushed his teeth, for example, and years later had to have a mouthful of fake ones installed. I might have been slightly aware that he was suffering, but I am ashamed to say that I never tried to understand why.

Mostly that was because I didn't want to be like him. I was the goodie two-shoes, the "good" kid, and wanted to keep it that way. Years later, when we finally talked, we realized that neither of us wanted to be like the other. He saw me as busting my rear end—good grades, friends, sports teams, cheerleading—trying to get my parents' love and approval, and never getting it. And I saw him failing—in school, with friends, at sports—and getting nothing but grief for that. Neither strategy worked. Neither of us got much love or approval.

In high school, a teacher or school counselor finally noticed something was wrong with my brother—who was chronically withdrawn, angry, and visibly unhappy—and referred him to a psychiatrist. As he explained to me years later, he spent the better part of a year in the doctor's office in sullen silence, then burst out with a homicidal rage so powerful the doctor recommended that he be sent away immediately to boarding school lest he kill my father. Luckily, there was no assault, no fight, no physical battle. I still have no idea how the psychiatrist managed to tell my parents that my brother needed to be removed from the house without inflaming or shaming my father. If the psychiatrist had been less skillful, there probably would have been violence. Still, it always bothered me: Why was my brother exiled and not my father?

At private school, though, my brother actually thrived. He never talked to me about how he felt about being out of the house, but it was clearly a good thing and a major turning point in his life. An inept athlete at home, he suddenly became an excellent skier and rock climber and a better student. He went on to college and an externally normal life, though to me, he never seemed to fully escape our father's dark shadow.

The tragedy that shaped my brother's life occurred when he was three.

It happened on one of those awful family camping trips we started taking as soon as my brother turned three. 1950. Just a few years after my father got out of the army and back from the war.

My father still had a lot of the army in him. I think he concocted those camping trips to turn us into little soldiers, though we never understood if that was why we couldn't call him "Dad." Maybe he thought children were miniature adults—people with small bodies but adult brains. Maybe he just didn't want to be a dad. He certainly was not fit to be one.

That summer, he dug out his old army gear—the canvas water bottle that got strapped to the front grill of the Ford so the airflow on the road would cool it. The big army-green gas can that he washed thoroughly and filled with water. The heavy canvas tent that could have held all four of us. My father had wanted privacy, though, so he also packed a small canvas pup tent for my brother and me.

In the car, we actually loved one thing my father did. He taught us old army songs like "When the Caissons Go Rolling Along" and "Over There." Singing in the car was one of the few times he lost the fierce look on his face. Sometimes, he even smiled.

Of course, we didn't understand all the words, especially "caissons." But it didn't matter. In those moments, we were mesmerized by my father's voice. When he belted out the bass part, his face, with its huge, shaggy, almost-touching eyebrows lost its usual strained look. I could never tell if it was the songs themselves or something deep inside him, but sometimes he would suddenly choke up and stop singing for a minute, as if he were about to cry. My brother and I would look at each other, not sure which was scarier, his anger or his tears.

Let the More Loving One Be Me

It was the end of summer, and we were on a big trip to Cape Breton Island, up in Nova Scotia. My mother explained that "Nova Scotia" meant "New Scotland," though we didn't even know there was an old Scotland. It had taken days to pack all the gear, the canned food, the Coleman stove, the blankets, the tents, the sweaters, the books.

To celebrate the adventure, my brother and I were each given a small plastic suitcase. My brother packed his with candy and small toys. I filled mine with comics. The suitcases—there were no child seats or even seat belts in those days—were placed on the back seat so we could sit on them and be high enough to see out the windows.

When we finally arrived in the campground at dusk, we had a quick dinner of beans, franks, and toasted marshmallows. Then my father told us we were old enough for a camping present: a jackknife for each of us. I was six. My brother was three. My brother's fingers were so small he had trouble using his fingernail to pull out the blade. Once he got it out, he needed help getting it folded back in.

"Just remember," said my father, "never cut upward. Only downward. And never run with the knife open." I understood and nodded. Copying me, my brother nodded, too.

After a week of smoky food and afternoons spent reading comics while rain pattered on the tent walls, it was time to pack up and take the car ferry back to Canada and get on the highway home. My brother and I sat on our little suitcases, watching the ferry pull out of the dock. A loudspeaker told us we would soon start the crossing from Cape Breton to Halifax.

Bored, my brother pulled his jackknife out of his pocket. He picked up a piece of string left on the back seat from the packing. He opened the knife, made a loop out of the string in his left hand, and holding the knife in his right hand, placed it, sharp edge up, under the loop.

"You're supposed to cut down," I whispered.

But he had already started the motion. As I watched, the knife cut the string and flew up, into his left eye. Surprised more than anything else, my brother didn't cry. Neither did I. I reached forward and tapped my mother hard on her shoulder. "He cut his eye. He was cutting up with his knife."

"I told him not to cut up," fumed my father, whirling around, hands almost flying off the steering wheel. He fell silent when he saw the knife sticking out of my brother's eye. My mother stared, then started crying.

"I told you he was too young to have a knife," she said, closing her mouth fast when she caught my father's expression. She shot me a "be quiet" look, but I didn't need to be told. I was numb.

Finally, my brother started to cry, though I couldn't quite tell whether it was from pain or shock or fear.

I was forgotten, and glad for it. I touched my eyes, covering each one in turn. Both still worked. I felt my own knife in my pocket, all closed up, the way it should be.

My father ran to find the ferry captain but came back a few minutes later saying, "They can't speed it up."

My brother and my mother were clinging to each other in the front seat. She was holding the knife in his eye because she thought it would bleed if she took it out. I sat silently in the back.

"They will have firemen waiting to take us to the hospital when we dock," said my father.

My mother wouldn't look at my father, but I stole a glance. Somehow, he seemed puffed up, as if having talked to the boat captain he was back in charge, having solved this difficult problem.

The firemen did meet us and rush us to the hospital. While the doctors operated on my brother, my mother, father, and I sat in plastic chairs in a hallway. Nobody had remembered to bring a book for me, so I eventually put my head on my mother's shoulder and closed my eyes.

It was very late when the doctors came out. I can still picture how gray and grim-faced they looked. "He may not lose his eye," I think one doctor said. "But if he keeps his vision, he will only see black and white."

We were finally allowed to go to my brother's bed, where a big white patch covered his left eye. He was asleep and, except for the patch, looked normal to me. My shoulders relaxed for the first time in hours.

We stayed in a hotel that night, with me sleeping on a little cot, my parents in the big bed, talking quietly. I gave up listening.

The next morning, we went back to the hospital to get my brother. I couldn't tell how he was feeling, whether he was scared or not. My parents decided that my brother and father would fly home while my mother and I would drive. I pretended to be the navigator, maps spread out on my lap. I think it was just my mother's way of distracting me since I never could tell exactly where we were.

When we got to New York, we went to meet my father and brother, who had gone right to the hospital, still in camping clothes. Once again, the doctors had to operate. Hours later, they emerged, looking no happier than the first doctors had.

"We had to take out the eye," said the head doctor grimly. "The eye socket was infected. We were afraid that if the optic nerve became infected, he would lose sight in the other eye too."

Several weeks later, my brother's eye socket had healed. I screwed up my six- year-old courage and looked. It was red, with lots of blood vessels that looked like tiny, squirming worms, very deep and very, very empty. He wore a patch over it, the patch too big for his little face.

One day, my father made my mother and me march around the house with a patch on one eye to see what it felt like to see out of only one eye as my brother had to do. That was the only processing of the trauma—no apologies, no cuddles, no family hugs. A life-altering event that was never spoken of again.

Eventually, my parents took my brother to get a glass eye. He howled as its hard edges rubbed his baby flesh. The eye fascinated me, though, partly because it didn't move from side to side like his other one. I tried to ask him questions about it, but he didn't seem to understand what was going on.

As he grew, my brother would go back every so often for new fake eyes. They all seemed too big, probably because it's usually adults, not kids, who lose their eyes and need new ones. Of course, it's usually adults, not kids, who have knives.

For me, it was always weird. None of the other kids I knew had to get glass eyes. Nobody else's brother had a fake eye. It soon became another family secret, another feeling of shame.

Over the decades, the fake eyes got more real-looking as the technology improved. But that left eye, the glass one, never stopped weeping. All his life, my brother had to mop it frequently with a tissue or his handkerchief. He always said it was just serum or some protective bodily fluid the eye socket secreted. Or allergies. Or a cold.

It probably was. But I always thought it was tears, the tears of a three-year-old boy whose father refused to be called "Dad."

ᏼMothers and Daughters

The Glass Shield

My mother seemed to live behind a big, glass shield
Visible and audible, but somehow always out of reach
Warm to strangers, but cool to me. Why?
I tried but never made it past
That shield, that barrier, that distance.
My child-self wailed, silently
So she wouldn't punish
My secret need
For her,
Unheard

I have spent years trying to understand that there was nobody home—nobody home outside me as a child, and nobody home inside me, either. I knew I had a mother, and yet, I didn't. Just a big, empty, loveless hole where connection and security were supposed to be.

Thanks to therapy, I've been able to trace the origins of that feeling to growing up with a mother I could see and hear and touch but not feel, a mother who *seemed* to be there but wasn't, a mother who was more comfortable throwing dinner parties than hugging children.

But it's not just therapy that has helped me understand myself. I've also given this question some serious study. In fact, I was on track for a PhD in psychology when I (happily) got diverted to journalism. Along the way, I've learned a lot about what's called attachment theory, thanks to authors such as David J. Wallin and Louis Cozolino and, of course, *New York Times* best-selling author Bessel van der Kolk, who wrote *The Body Keeps the Score—Brain, Mind, and Body in the Healing of Trauma.*

I've also dug into less academic but equally thought-provoking popular books like *Daughters Betrayed by Their Mothers* by Holli Kenley, a California psychologist and author, and *Daughter Detox* by Peg Streep, a *Psychology Today* blogger and author.

The titles alone are shocking. The idea that someone might have to "detox" from a mother? The idea that daughters can be betrayed by the very person who is supposed to nurture them and make them feel safe and secure? It all sounds so blaming, so hostile, so unforgiving. Not to mention so politically incorrect. It wasn't so long ago, back in the 1930s, that psychiatrists actually used terms like "schizophrenogenic mother," the false idea that a mother who was cold, rejecting, distant, and/or overprotective was the cause of schizophrenia in her child, not a combination of genes and other factors. Not exactly music to a feminist's ears.

Indeed, blaming mothers for many if not most psychological problems in their offspring was a staple in psychology for decades. More recently, thanks to the women's movement, we have gotten partially out from under that negative view of women in their roles as mothers.

And yet . . . and yet. There is also abundant evidence that when a mother doesn't provide enough love and security for her child, that child can end up insecure if there aren't substitute nurturers around. From an evolutionary standpoint, a secure attachment is essential for a mammalian infant's survival. And that's especially true for human babies who, unlike dogs or cats or elephants, can't walk or crawl to get their own food or avoid predators.

Obviously, the bond between an adult woman and her infant daughters and sons is complex, a relationship that psychiatrists and psychologists have been exploring since pivotal work in the late 1960s by John Bowlby and Mary Ainsworth, and later, by others in the field of attachment theory. (The first studies of attachment theory, interestingly, were not about mothers and daughters but about English boys sent off to private schools at a very young age. Boys need their mothers, too.)

According to attachment theory, the key to well-being, regardless of the gender of the child, is a secure primary bond—the deeper the attachment, the better. Developing this bond involves a kind of dance of attunement, with mother and baby rejoicing in gazing at each other, mirroring each other's movements, tracing each other's faces, memorizing the sound of each other's voices.

When there is a healthy, strong, secure attachment between a mother and infant, the baby can go on to explore and engage with others, knowing her mother is always there to come back to. Sure, a securely attached infant may get fussy and agitated when the mother leaves, but she quickly calms down and snuggles when the mother comes back. In other words, the mother is reliable, a safe haven that the baby learns she can always rely on. The mother is really, truly, warmly *there*.

On the other hand, with insecure attachments, babies often show significant fear when a stranger shows up, even if the mother is present. Insecurely attached babies can't relax and respond to the mother's attempts at interaction when she does come back after a short absence. They may even refuse to be held or hit the mother when she approaches.

The insecure attachment problem is compounded by the fact that a very young child has no words to describe her feelings of anxiety or abandonment. If the mother can't tune in to her baby's emotional and physical feelings and put words to them, the baby has no way to understand her own feelings. When a mother *can* empathically resonate with the child's internal state and translate that state into words, the child learns to associate feelings with words. Not only does this help a child feel less helpless in the face of strong feelings, but this pairing of feelings with words helps the brain form networks that link language and emotion.

With all the recent achievements in neurobiology, it's now clear that specific hormones are involved with attachment too. The warm, positive feelings in a healthy mother-infant bond are facilitated by hormones that enhance the feeling of connection— oxytocin, prolactin, endorphins, and dopamine. These hormones in turn go on to trigger brain development in a way that further promotes emotional attachment.

In fact, fascinating studies of other primates show that when a mother-infant pair engages in mutual touching or grooming, *both* animals show increases in levels of endorphins, the naturally occurring "feel good" hormones. And if the animals are given naltrexone (a drug that *blocks* the effects of endorphins), the animals stop trying to be near each other—strong evidence of how important these bonding hormones are for connectedness.

And when all this wonderful stuff doesn't happen? Or happens inconsistently? Or unreliably? It's knowing that you have a mother but you don't.

The little girl scooped up some pebbles, put a handful in her pocket, then, ever so delicately—not hard like a boy—threw them underhand, one by one, into Rockport Harbor. Her mother, a pretty woman in a yellow sun hat (to prevent more freckles) and with a loaf of fresh-baked Anadama bread tucked in her straw shopping basket, stood nearby, seemingly lost in thought. Her coral-colored toenails peeked out through the straps of her sandals.

Mothers and Daughters

"Are you watching, Mom?" asked the little girl.

"Of course, dear," said her mother as she looked past the girl to the small boats bobbing near the wharf. "But we have to go soon."

The girl, sturdy little legs tanned golden by the summer sun, blonde curls a salty mass under her Red Sox cap, turned away from her mother and tossed a whole handful of pebbles into the sea, all at once, overhand, a little too hard.

"Nicely, dear, nicely," said her mother absent-mindedly, swiveling her head back and forth. Her mother seemed to always be looking for her husband, or, when she found him, to be looking around nervously for ways to keep him calm and under control.

The girl went to her mother's side, wrapped her arms as far as they would reach around her mother's hips, and hung on tightly. She wanted to ask, "Do you love me?" but didn't. She understood, little as she was, that somehow it was her job to take care of her mother, not the other way around, especially when her father was present. So she nuzzled her head against her mother's hip, seeking comfort by giving it.

The midday sun was hot, but the girl felt little warmth from her mother's body. You can't get something that is not there. Or maybe there was something there. Nothing as clear as a shudder, more like a hole inside the mother, an absence. The girl let her mother's not-there-ness seep into her own body. The shared empty feeling somehow bound them together, the tenuous connection better than no connection at all. She squeezed her mother more tightly.

The mother looked down and patted the girl's head absently through the baseball cap.

"We have to go now, dear." The girl detached herself and reached for her mother's hand, but found only the shopping basket.

"Come along, now. We're late."

On May 25, 2020, I was as shocked as anyone when Minneapolis police officer Derek Chauvin killed George Floyd by kneeling on his neck for almost ten minutes. Floyd, a forty-six-year-old Black man with five children, had bought some cigarettes with what a store clerk thought was a counterfeit $20 bill. The clerk called the cops. The cops pulled a gun on Floyd. After initially cooperating, Floyd resisted being put into a police car. Then, as dramatic cell phone video showed, Chauvin knelt on Floyd's neck as three other officers stood and watched.

The sheer brutality, the racism, the injustice, and the horror were seared into my brain. But something else was too. In his agony, Floyd did something I was shocked to realize I probably would not have done. He cried out for his mother.

George Floyd

George Floyd died. The Black man who'd done nothing wrong.
He cried for his mother, a cry for help
And safety and protection, for love and life.
Who would I cry for in extremis?
Not her, the stiff-armed one
Who said babies scared her.
I was her baby,
She, too scared
To love
Me

ॐ

My mother died in my arms. It was the closest moment we ever had.

I had been with her for the last three weeks of her life. I kept her company, took her beloved poodles for walks, fixed dinner, combed her hair, applied her makeup, and gave her medications. We "played jewelry," admiring and trying on her favorite pieces, each one accompanied by a story of who had given it to her and on what occasion. As always in her presence, I was who I was supposed to be—the smiling, competent, dutiful, loving daughter. On the outside.

Mothers and Daughters

Inside, despite the passage of decades, there still lived a little girl—sometimes an infant, sometimes a three-year-old, sometimes a five-year-old. But a child, a hungry child, a child who was always missing something she could never quite define or find. A little girl always searching and aching for something—intimacy—that this woman, now dying so gracefully, had never given. Or, more charitably, had probably never had to give in the first place.

When I realized the end was near, I took a leave from work and drove to her house in Connecticut. I planned to remain for as long as it would take. When I got there, someone—my brother, I think—told her I had arrived.

"Is that my beautiful daughter?" I heard her ask.

"Me? She really thinks I'm beautiful? She loves me?" I was stunned.

All these years, I had never been sure of her love. She was physically there, of course. She was pretty, gracious, charming, but underneath all the glamour, she was empty. All I knew, as she once told me, was that babies scared her. When she once caught me breastfeeding my infant son, she fled, saying that breastfeeding was "barbaric." Intimacy was no easier as I grew up; in fact, it was harder as I gradually tried to express my feelings. She couldn't understand. Eventually, I stopped trying.

I had had a shocking moment one day during a massage. The massage therapist happened to be a professional singer. She offered me an unusual bonus: At the end of the regular massage, she would sing to me. I had never heard of such a thing but accepted eagerly. She turned off the spa music, dimmed the lights further, and cradled my face in her warm hands.

In a soft, alto voice, she hummed, then sang the sweetest, most tender baby-love song. Lullabies to my innermost self. The tears began. I couldn't stop them and didn't try. They streamed down my face onto her hands.

She continued to sing, without hesitation or remarking on my tears. She was singing to me! I had never felt this way before but knew with certainty what the feeling was: Mother love! A thought quickly followed:

Let the More Loving One Be Me

That's what I never had. That is what I was always missing. So simple, so complex.

The massage therapist, someone to whom I still feel grateful, told me afterward that while I was getting dressed, she went out into the hallway. She was so moved by what had happened between us that she wept in the arms of a fellow therapist.

How does a child learn to construct a self, a life, with that missing foundation? How does one learn to feel safe if the ground underneath is constantly shaking, unreliable? The self becomes a scaffolding, jury-rigged around a toddler longing to be held. Who does the holding if the mother or the father does not?

As the days in Connecticut ticked by and our vigil continued, I did not speak of the yearning two-year-old still buried deep inside me. I did not bring up all the other things that had kept us at a distance for all these years—my father's rages, his drinking, her prioritization of him over my brother and me, her abandoning us the minute he walked in the door.

He was always the important one—not me, not my brother, not even her. She was proud of sticking by him for fifty-four years. She was proud of telling the world how romantic their marriage was, how wonderful and brilliant he was. This was her truth, and was to the end, even as she instructed me firmly not to bury her ashes with his. Enough was enough. Apparently, fifty-four years of wedded together-ness was okay. Eternity was not.

About a week before her death, I told my mother one night that she looked pretty. She didn't believe me. "My mother," she told me, "said, 'You will never be pretty. But you can at least be tidy.'"

"But you are pretty," I said to no avail.

There was nothing I could say. Mother messages endure.

Toward the very end, I began to get restless, eager to return home, to work, to my life. The hospice nurse took me aside.

"She's close now. Don't go."

I returned to the bed and took my mother in my arms. Her two

32

black poodles snuggled in. At last, I told myself, I was the one she wanted. I allowed myself to feel chosen, honored.

Every time she exhaled, I said softly, "You're okay. Everyone you love is okay. You can let go." Childbirth in reverse. I timed my statements to her breathing, even as her breaths became farther apart. The dogs snuggled closer. I tightened my arms around her.

Breath. "It's okay, Mom. Everything is okay. You are safe."

Breath. "I love you." Breath. "I love you." Breath. "I love you."

Then, no more breaths. Gone.

Had she ever really been there?

I watched as the undertakers put my mother on a gurney, carried her downstairs, and wheeled her to the waiting van. I went back to the still-warm bed and called the poodles to me. They were inconsolable. They had lost their mother.

And had I? Yes, but that was a long time ago.

ᶜMy World Expands

T he unhappy family chains began to loosen a bit when, at seventeen, I won a chance to spend the summer in Denmark as an American Field Service exchange student. I lived with a Danish family with three daughters. The oldest daughter, Lena, took me to Tivoli, the fabulous amusement park in the center of Copenhagen, on my first night there. Even that first evening was an eye-opener. I was stunned to see girls my age holding hands and walking around with unshaved legs and armpits. A naïf from suburban Pelham, NY, I knew nobody in Pelham who would dare leave the house that way.

Living with my Danish family was a shock too, and a good one. My three Danish sisters and my Danish mother, "Mor," and father, "Far," actually liked each other. Nobody drank too much. Nobody was angry. We had five meals a day, counting afternoon tea before dinner and evening tea several hours after dinner. (In fact, dinner preparation took place even as the cleanup from afternoon tea was still going on.) People laughed. We all teased our youngest sister, Gertie, who took it all in good spirits. They even teased me good-naturedly, especially when all four of us sisters went horseback riding.

I'd never ridden horses before, much less galloped, terrified, hair flying, on a beach, the horse's feet splashing in the shallow water. To this day, the words, "*Skal vi galloppere?*" ("Shall we gallop?") make me shudder. It was wonderful, though. For the first time in my young life, I felt relaxed and safe in a family.

That life-expanding summer also provided my first, albeit unwitting, foray into what would be my life's work.

It was an inauspicious start to a journalism career.

I was seventeen. So was everybody else (except the long-suffering crew) crammed aboard the SS Seven Seas.

The Seven Seas (widely rumored to be condemned as unseaworthy) was carrying seven hundred of us—American Field Service (AFS) students all—heading home from a summer living with European host families. We were happy, considerably fatter than when we had left the US three months earlier, and full of newly discovered sophistication.

We boarded the ship through the gangway and, still carrying our bags, stopped to see the bulletin board, jostling to read the dozens of handwritten signs.

"Editor needed for daily shipboard newspaper," read one.

I could do that, I thought. But I was a girl, and girls were not editors, or so I assumed. I turned to the mousy-looking boy standing next to me.

"Wanna do this?" I asked. "I will if you will."

"Sure," he said, and off we went, snaking our way up one dark shipboard stairway and down another looking for the "newsroom," a microscopic cubbyhole with a couple of worn chairs; reams of waiting, blank paper; and a very old, balky mimeograph machine.

We plopped down on the chairs and eyed each other. The boy—whose name I can't remember now and barely could during our entire ten-day voyage—had absolutely no journalism experience.

I had written a few saccharine "letters from Denmark" to my hometown paper, the Pelham Sun, raving about the pastries and my host family and offering sophomoric insights into world affairs. I had also written for my high school newspaper—more saccharine features about hunky football players and a fast-track star we called "The Flying Finn."

Let the More Loving One Be Me

We decided to be a daily. We didn't seem to have a boss or supervisor of any sort. And we clearly had no competition. Nobody else seemed to have answered the ad on the bulletin board.

So we wrote silly stuff, pieces about the food on board. We listed the scheduled shipboard activities. We reported on the weather. We wrote jokes about how rickety the ship seemed and features about the countries we had visited. Bland, but blissful. I had never been happier. I spent the days covered in mimeograph ink, thrilled to pass out our daily efforts and watch as people gathered in small groups to read them.

I would hardly have called myself an investigative reporter, but about halfway through the trip, I stumbled upon a shocker: Some of the AFS-ers confided that they had become very friendly with their host nationals. Even the girls hinted that they had had sex with boys from the countries they visited.

I was from Pelham, for heaven's sake. Nobody had sex in Pelham. I went to church. I was in the choir. I was a bellringer. I was a Girl Scout. I was a cheerleader. I didn't drink. I didn't swear. I more or less got straight As. I was an AFS student. I was working for world peace! And they were having sex?

I also had access to a mimeograph machine. So, in the heat of passion, I wrote an editorial fiercely lambasting my fellow students for tarnishing the image of AFS and Americans abroad. Who did they think they were, messing around, breaking the rules, ruining our mission? We were the force for good, for purity. We were the youth of America, the future of the world. What were these kids thinking?

Fueled by the outrage of the naïve, I went on and on in what I assumed was a well-written, much-needed piece. (Much to my relief, I no longer have a copy.) When I ran out of steam, my co-editor read the editorial, didn't say much, picked a phrase from my piece, and slapped it on as a headline: "The Lousy Few." I cranked up the mimeograph machine, handed out the copies, and went to dinner, aglow with righteous fervor. I was so right, they, so wrong.

Back in my cabin, my roommates, despite my showing up every

night covered in mimeograph ink, didn't seem to suspect that I was the editor. They read the editorial and cracked up. Laughter? That was the last thing I expected. This was serious. I was serious. And suddenly, scared. I announced that I was seasick, asked them to bring me some soup, and hid under the covers.

The next morning, I tried to sneak back to the newsroom. People might know my name, but they didn't know my face. When I got to the dining room, I bumped into a huge parade of kids carrying a banner made from a bedsheet.

"The Lousy Few!" it proclaimed proudly. The students were having a ball. They shouted, pumped their fists, and sang, "The Lousy Few! The Lousy Few!" They also yelled that they were going to find and torture whoever had written that editorial.

Mortified and stunned at the depth of my own naivete, I was also suddenly aware of a new feeling. I was ecstatic that people had actually read what I'd written. I was in awe. I could move people with my words! What power!

I skulked away from the demonstration, eventually making it back to the "newsroom."

"They actually read this stuff!" I said to my coeditor. He shrugged. We vowed to keep putting out the paper for the rest of the trip. I kept faking seasickness whenever I was in the cabin, and never told my cabinmates I was the editor. I hid my purple, ink-stained clothes.

Today, more than sixty years, numerous journalism awards, and several books later, I'm still amazed that I can move people with my words. And that I can have so much fun doing it.

In the early fall of 1962, my parents dropped me, my duffel bags, and my dreams off at the entrance to Shafer Hall. I took to Wellesley immediately, though I had applied there for a less than lofty reason: I wanted to marry a Harvard man. (I ended up marrying two.)

The campus, of course, was beautiful: trees, hills, a lake, old-fashioned buildings, a bell tower that worked. I was in heaven.

Let the More Loving One Be Me

Young women, sometimes accompanied by young men, walked the pathways, carrying books and hope.

And, as it turned out, an all-women's school was perfect for me, the ideal antidote to my sexist upbringing. My family didn't value women, but Wellesley sure did. What a shock! Women counted. Women mattered. I must matter, too. My classmates actually had plans, real plans, for doing something with their lives. They— we—were good at things. They—we—spoke up in class, unafraid of being silenced by male classmates. We were a living example of what Matina Horner, who would soon become the sixth president of another women's college, Radcliffe, postulated was a huge problem for many girls and women: the fear of success, the idea that women often failed because they were afraid that succeeding would make them unfeminine and unattractive to men. Not at Wellesley, thank God. Not at Wellesley.

My roommate, Karen, was a brilliant California girl who'd skipped a few grades, didn't know much more about the world than I did, and became a nationally known medical ethicist. Down the hall lived Sally, a Quaker from Pennsylvania who became a prominent anthropologist and my lifelong best friend. Another classmate, Diana Chapman Walsh, went on to become president of Wellesley College. Others became physicians, college professors, social workers, business leaders.

And almost, president of the United States.

Okay, Hillary Clinton wasn't exactly a classmate. We did overlap for one year, but I didn't know her personally. But, oh! How connected I would feel that election night in 2016!

Dear Hillary,
    It's all my fault. I'm so sorry.
    I opened the bottle of champagne before the polls closed.
    "This isn't going to jinx anything, right?" I asked my husband, Ken, as he poured the drinks.

My World Expands

"Nah," he said, clinking my glass. "She'll win."

I was so ready to party. I had been a happy wreck all day. I'd missed a turn on the way to an appointment. I'd driven over to pick up the dog at doggie day care, forgetting that she was in the van to come home. I'd been all thumbs at the gym trying to set my Polar heart rate monitor for a quick workout on the treadmill. Any attempt at working had long since flown out the window. I'd spent the afternoon getting ready for the big event at Wellesley College at eight that night.

Hillary, we, your fellow alums (I was '66, you were '69) had gotten the word: Wear white, in honor of the suffragettes, our fore-sisters. Not so easy, finding white in November, but Target came through at $29.95 for a pair of white jeans. They would have fit . . . five pounds ago. No matter. Getting dressed, I felt like a bride—a lacey, new white bra, white camisole, white pearls, the full Wellesley.

The Sports Center, which hadn't been there when I was a student, was filling up as I arrived. Balloons everywhere. T-shirt-clad students handed out Mardi Gras–style necklaces of red, white, and blue. Other students passed out popcorn and paper flags on little wooden sticks proclaiming, "Making the Impossible Possible." A souvenir table sold mugs proudly proclaiming, "Madam President—Get Used to It"—and T-shirts with "Wellesley women run for . . ." on the front, and "President" on the back. The students were so young and bright-eyed. Was I ever that young? (I had just been to my fiftieth reunion.)

High-top food tables were laid out with delicious-looking *hors d'oeuvres*. The line for wine grew behind me as I snagged my glass. Purple scarf around my neck, I looked for other alums in purple, my class color. There they were, chatting excitedly around one of the little round tables that identified alumnae by decade. I found the sign beckoning to me like a magnet: "1960s."

Cell phones in hand, purple-scarved classmates snapped group selfies, exchanged emails with the obligatory, "Of course, I'll send these to you."

The room filled until we were packed, not quite elbow to elbow, but a solid female mass, occasional males dotting the crowd like sprinkles on a cupcake. On the huge screen at the front, famous alums—Diane Sawyer, Lynn Sher—radiated joy and pride in Hillary, our Hillary, Wellesley. The first woman president! One of ours. One of us. It was going to happen!

That wonderful female energy that never fails to explode when women come together feeling their—our—collective power swept palpably through the room, a tidal wave of anticipation.

Ninety-six years after we had won the right to vote in America, ninety-eight years after the British suffragettes held hunger strikes for that basic right, we were—tonight!—going to break through that final glass ceiling. It was going to happen tonight!

Hillary, we are so proud of you. So exquisitely proud of you. You are us! You hold our hearts! We have been with you, every step of the way! We are one. We are women. Hear us roar!!

The room fell quiet. New Hampshire was tottering. Florida— the Latinos, the Latinas—wavered. Ohio. Michigan. Wisconsin.

Silence. Our faces revealed the truth before words did. No roars now. Not anything. This was not supposed to happen. This was to be the historic night. The night women were second class no more. Yet here we stood—stunned, silent, willing that big map on the screen to turn blue, Wellesley blue.

Hillary, we tried so hard. We gave you everything we had: time, money, energy, love. And you tried so hard, with every ounce of your being. For many of us in that cavernous hall, you were our best chance to see a woman in the White House before we die.

A few hours from now, tomorrow morning (will there be a tomorrow?) you will give the most beautiful, heartfelt speech of your life. You will speak directly to young girls, urging them never to give up. They won't. We won't. We promise.

We will eventually take heart from the fact that you did get the most votes, by three million. You actually won! That's huge.

So, courage to you, Hillary. And to us.

My World Expands

I'm still sorry about that too-early glass of champagne. But why let it go to waste? I'll drink the rest, with a toast to you, my Madam President.

Love, Judy

Of course, Wellesley was about more than studying hard enough to make Phi Beta Kappa and leaving my parents' heartless Republican world behind. It was about falling in love. Fast and hard.

Early in the fall of freshman year, I went with some Wellesley pals to one of the first mixers with Harvard freshmen. I spotted a tall, handsome guy standing next to a shorter, bespectacled one. Feeling frisky and flirtatious, I sauntered over to the tall one and, as I remember it, asked him what time it was.

As he would always recall it, with a wink, my line was a bit saucier: "Do you have the time?" Whatever I said, he said yes. And that was the beginning of four years of fun. I went to Harvard classes with him sometimes, and, as Matina Horner could have predicted, was struck by how the men talked and the women didn't. I helped him write his papers. He was a swimmer, so I went to endless swim meets, sweating in the humid stands, and to football games, freezing through endless plays in my pantyhose and heels, bladder full and hands icy.

The years flew by. We got "pinned." We got engaged. Graduation loomed. It was a photo finish.

His roommates called him "The Bod," and with good reason. At an impressive six feet four inches, Bruce was captain of the Harvard swim team, a gifted breaststroker with a gap-toothed grin and 220 pounds of gorgeous muscle. Handsome and charming, he had swum his way into Harvard, and into my heart.

On this sunny June day, however, none of that mattered.

Bruce was in his dorm room, pacing, gnawing at what was left of his nails. We were twenty-two years old, getting married in a week. But first, he had to graduate. Which meant winding up with a C average.

Which meant getting a B+ in music. Which meant passing the music exam. Today. Which seemed highly unlikely.

It's not that Bruce wasn't musical, though he wasn't. It was that he had mere hours to comprehend the structure of a symphony. This could have been mastered weeks before, of course, but studying was not Bruce's strong point.

So, there he was, in shorts, a T-shirt, and bare feet, "skimming" a symphony by putting the needle from the record player onto the record at various spots trying to find the A theme, the B theme, etc. It was not going well.

My job that day, having graduated from Wellesley a few days earlier, was to drive Bruce's beloved but balky MG to a foreign auto parts dealer out on Route 16. The car was jammed with my college books, clothes, posters, and, somewhere amid the piles, my sentimental favorite: a little white plastic box with the eighty-nine-cent "diamond" ring Bruce had given me while we waited for my real engagement ring to be sized. (This process had not been straightforward, either. To get the money for the real ring, Bruce had had to sell his semifunctional motorcycle. Not surprisingly, buyers had proved scarce.)

I had to get to the auto dealer today because unless we got the fuel pump fixed, we would not be able to drive the MG to our wedding in New York. Bruce had given me detailed instructions on how to fix the thing—I had to take a bobby pin and stick it in just the right place to keep something open (or was it closed?) so that gas (or was it air?) could get to wherever it was supposed to go so the car would run.

This was actually working pretty well. I only had to stop every block or so, pull over, open the trunk (for some reason, the fuel pump was in the back in vintage MGs), jiggle the bobby pin, get back in, and drive another block. I was feeling pretty proud of myself.

As I headed west on Storrow Drive, it began to rain. I drove slowly around the big curve of the Charles across from 1010 Memorial Drive. When the fuel pump conked out again, it did so with alarming finality. I guided the dying car over to the side of the road and skidded to a stop on the wet, slippery grass at the top of a slight incline. I put the car in neutral, as I thought I was supposed to, jerked on the emergency brake, got out, and headed around to the trunk. Out of the corner of my eye, I saw a guy in a station wagon pull over onto the grass near me.

Suddenly, the car started rolling. I grabbed the door handle on the driver's side, pulling as hard as I could. (Not very effectively—I only weighed 110 pounds.) The car began to slide slowly by me. As it gathered speed, I let go, ran around to the back, and grabbed the fender. I held on for all I was worth, then lost my footing, breaking one of my thong sandals. When I began slipping under the car, I let go.

Faster now, the car glided toward the river, launching itself into the murky brown water. It stayed afloat for a good twenty feet. Then the front end dove under, sleek as a seal. The back wheels and undercarriage rose straight up, the license plate high in the sky. The car seemed to pause there, frozen in time. Suddenly, the back end sank. An enormous brown bubble almost the size of the car—the Charles was very polluted in those days—burped up, then ebbed away.

Nothing. Not even a ripple.

"You poor girl," said the guy from the station wagon, who came to stand by me. "Your car just disappeared."

"I know."

We stared at the blank water in silence.

"This is surreal," he said.

"I know. My fiancé is going to be pissed."

With my red granny dress plastered to my body from the rain and my hair sodden, I had a moment of manic abandon. With one sandal already broken, I threw it and the other one into the water, where they floated upside-down.

"I never really liked that car," I said. The guy from the station wagon just looked at me.

With a final glance at the now-placid river, we got into his car. He took me to Bruce's dorm.

"Good luck." He waved.

"I'll need it."

With old-fashioned parietal hours still in effect—females were not allowed into men's dorms except for certain times of day—I asked another student to get Bruce for me.

He galloped downstairs, perplexed.

"Hi, sweetie," I began. "You'll never guess where the car is."

Perplexity turned to panic. "Where?"

"Kind of on the bottom of the Charles. But we can just leave it there, at least until your exam is over. It'll be fine. We can get it later."

"No!" he hollered.

"What about your exam?"

"I don't care," he said, turning to run upstairs for his shoes and his wallet.

We ran (not easy for me, barefoot) across the bridge and down to the spot where the car had been, now abuzz with dozens of police cars and news trucks. Someone from 1010 Memorial Drive had seen the car go into the water, thought it was a suicide, and called the cops. When the cops—and the reporters—saw the floating sandals, it confirmed their worst fears.

"It's my car. I'm okay!" I yelled. But two policemen were already in the water, bashing at the car windows. Somehow, they got a door open. My books, posters, clothes, and fake diamond in the little plastic box began to drift downriver, my life slipping by before my eyes. And, as it turned out, before the eyes of thousands of viewers watching TV.

Eventually, realizing that no one was in the car, the cops, dripping, climbed out of the murk.

"I'm the driver. I'm okay. I'm so sorry, I'm so sorry," I kept saying, explaining what had happened. The cops shook their heads. They could have drowned trying to save me. They could have bled to death from the gashes on their arms. (They did end the day at Mass General getting tetanus shots and stitches.)

A reporter, also rather soggy from the rain, approached, microphone in hand, TV camera rolling.

My World Expands

"Here's your ring! We saved your ring," he said. Little did I know—I wasn't a journalist yet—how reporters thought. The ring wound up as the headline on the evening news.

To the extent that I was thinking at all, I had planned to keep this episode secret from my mother, who was already hysterical over wedding details. She wasn't a romantic, but she was in full-time mother-of-the-bride mode—caterers, florists, photographers, clothes, decorations, things I barely knew or cared much about.

No luck. Her friends saw the news in New York and began calling her, delightedly embellishing the story with their assessments of how the bride-to-be looked. (Wet, shoeless, and miserable.)

By the time the tow truck arrived, my lingering hopes of letting the car rest in peace in its watery grave were dashed. Fastening their hooks to the car, the operators slowly hauled it out, a task made more difficult by the fact that the cops had left all four doors wide open. I stayed with the car as it was towed to a garage.

Bruce, meanwhile, ran back to his room, kept skimming the symphony, miraculously passed his exam, and graduated. The wedding went smoothly—my father behaved, my mother survived, nobody got too drunk—and we were finally Mr. and Mrs.

We spent the summer in wedded bliss with gallons of Mr. Clean and rolls of paper towels cleaning up the car, aiming to sell it by Labor Day to an unsuspecting freshman.

We did.

Shortly after graduation, Bruce and I joined the Peace Corps. To this day, I have no idea how this plan came about, though it was one of the best decisions I ever made. We just seemed to spend hours during senior year looking at Peace Corps material, thinking about different countries, and somehow, picking Brazil.

We started our Peace Corps training in Brattleboro, Vermont. On the very first day, we and the thirty-odd other members of our group were shuffled into classrooms and addressed by one of the charming language teachers who turned us, by the time our training was over three months later, into passable Portuguese speakers.

"*Bom dia, Teresa, como vai você?*" our teacher said.

We looked at each other, shrugged. She waved her arms. Clearly, we were supposed to repeat what she said. We did. Sort of. She started again. It was pure memory. No grammar books. No diagrammed sentences. No translations. Just words. The way a baby learns a language.

"*Eu me chamo Lisabete,*" she went, pointing dramatically to herself. Gradually, we caught on. When we got to "Lisabete," at first we imitated that, then realized we were supposed to substitute our own names.

And so on, for six, seven hours a day. All inductive learning. All sound and syllables. I loved every minute. Just before our group set off for Brazil, we all took a standard State Department language test; as a group, we did quite well, averaging a 2.5 out of 5. (By the end of our three years in Brazil, I had become quite fluent, not just speaking but also thinking and dreaming in Portuguese. At our final language exam, though, while the young man next to me got a perfect 5, I got a 4++ instead of a 5 because they had never, they said, given a 5 to a girl.)

Peace Corps training was intense but also, aside from the ever-present worry about "deselection"—flunking out for failing to learn Portuguese, failing to bond with other volunteers, or other, more amorphous sins—enormous fun. (In fact, our group bonded so well that in 2022, fifty-six years after we met, we had the latest in a series of reunions.)

Our most memorable moment in training, though, was the day we faced the dreaded chicken test.

I could feel the poor chicken's pulse in my left hand, nice and steady, unsuspecting, frighteningly full of life. I had it by the feet, its head dangling by my wobbly knees.

My World Expands

I stood somewhere in the middle in a long line of nervous Peace Corps trainees, all looking much more miserable than the upside-down chickens we clutched. It was late summer, 1966, a dreary day in Vermont. Bruce and I were twenty-two. We were newlyweds, armed with nothing but our relationship, our still-shiny rings, and safely stowed diplomas. We were ready to save the world and have fun doing it.

We'd passed every test the Peace Corps could throw at us—medical exams, physical fitness tests, language tests, history-of-Brazil tests, even psychological interviews (in which one just-married female volunteer was asked if she had any trouble reaching orgasm, though why this was a requirement for Peace Corps service we never figured out).

Today was the final test, and the toughest. We each had to kill a chicken—the right way, with an ax, although holding it by the head tightly and flinging it around and around until its head separated from its body so you could fling the body away with flourish was also an accepted method. It did not escape me that this slow-motion murder was a silly hurdle for the "Peace" Corps.

I had never killed anything before. Well, except that gerbil. And the chipmunk. The gerbil met its end one afternoon when I spied it scurrying around the dining room floor, screamed, and watched in horror as it fell onto its back, rigid, quite dead, all four feet sticking up in the air. I slid a record album cover under it and dumped it in the toilet.

As for the chipmunk, it had had the poor judgment to run out into a New Hampshire dirt road where I was jogging just as I was in midair, with neither foot on the ground and no control over where I landed. The little guy had a squishy end to its tiny life.

Those killings were accidents. Today's was pointless, premeditated murder. We were headed to Sao Paulo, one of the biggest cities in the world, where the need to kill chickens to feed ourselves was nonexistent. But deselection loomed for anyone too "chicken" to do the deed.

We had tried everything we could to get out of it. Barney, one of our more outspoken volunteers, had mobilized us to collective resistance with the formation of CLUCK, the Committee to Liquidate Uncouth Chicken Killers. He called WBZ radio in Boston, hoping for coverage of our incipient rebellion. We made CLUCK banners. We were psyched. But WBZ never showed, and our rebellion fizzled soon thereafter.

My turn came. The lead executioner gave me an ax and showed me how to hold it in my right hand. A wooden post about three feet high, flat on top, with two three-inch nails sticking up stood menacingly in front of me. The idea was to swing the chicken with the left hand so that its head was on one side of the nails, pull it by its feet to stretch out its neck, keep just the right amount of tension on the bird, hold it steady, and then, with one large swoop with the right hand, slam the ax squarely onto the exposed neck. One attempt was considered classy; two, torture.

My immediate future, and in my loftier thoughts, the future of the world I was hoping to save, flashed before me. What would happen if I couldn't kill the damned chicken but my husband could? Would my brand-new husband go to Brazil and leave me here, a deselected wife? Would we both stay behind and have to figure out quickly what to do with our lives without a Brazilian interlude to mercifully postpone adulthood?

I had, I regret to say, no moral qualms about killing the chicken. I felt no sadness, no empathy. How do you identify with a chicken anyway? A dog, yes, a cat, sure, a monkey, of course. But a chicken?

I did it, with the ax, in one committed swing. Pride. Blood. Shame. Then, holding the body of the chicken, still in my left hand, I looked around at the field we were in. All I could see were dozens of newly headless chickens running around crazily, wobbling, staggering, falling down. Shaking, I flung my chicken into the fray, elated that this trial was over.

Except it wasn't.

We each had to find our chicken (the headless birds, of course, all looked alike), take it inside a shed containing big vats of boiling water, dip the chicken in to loosen its feathers, then pluck out all the feathers—a tiring, grim job. Still not done, we then had to push our fingers in through the chicken's "vent," grab hold of its innards, and yank them out.

Then, finally, rest. And dinner.

Which, of course, was chicken.

Just before Christmas in 1966, our group departed for Brazil, with one final dramatic moment for Bruce. The Peace Corps doctors decided that we should all get a gamma globulin shot to boost our immunity for the inevitable diseases we were about to face in Brazil. We all lined up, exposed the relevant part of our anatomy, winced, and marched on to the plane. Except Bruce. The biggest guy in the group by at least thirty pounds, he dutifully got the shot in his butt and promptly fell over in a dead faint. Most of the group, except me, thought it was hilarious.

The Peace Corps hierarchy, at least in Brazil, was not the most organized. In fact, we thought it was pretty dumb of the Peace Corps to send all of us off to Brazil just days before Christmas, when the whole country was more or less shut down, we knew nobody except each other, and the hot, humid weather was utterly un-Christmas-y. Still, we coped. Our whole group took the bus from the city of Sao Paulo, where we were officially stationed, to the city of Santos, on a little island off the coast, Sao Vincente. We ate, drank, swam, and got through Christmas together.

Back on the mainland, our group was supposed to do what was called "urban community development." Nobody in the Peace Corps, or our host liaisons, seemed to know exactly what this meant. So, weirdly, despite my absurdly lofty intention to save the world and work for peace, I was assigned to teach gymnastics to middle-class ladies in a small city called Campinas in the state of Sao Paulo. Bruce was supposed to do something, nobody ever clarified exactly what, with the ragamuffin kids who worked as shoeshine boys.

Let the More Loving One Be Me

It didn't take us long to realize that this was not what we'd come for. We had to create our own jobs. I tactfully resigned from the gymnastics class—no one seemed to care—and started four Girl Scout troops—*Bandeirantes* in Portuguese—two troops in each of the government-built low-income housing projects in town, about a hundred girls in all. My goal was to provide fun, lead discussions of the cultural differences between Brazil and the United States, and generally help them and their families.

They danced around the corner of Vila Rica, the dusty, still-unpaved housing development in Campinas, Sao Paulo, Brazil, singing lustily, their blue uniforms—sewn the day before by their mothers—swishing around their legs, dark arms swinging in rhythm, brown faces alight.

Spotting me, they broke ranks and rushed forward, engulfing me in excited Portuguese. "Dona Judite! Olha!" Miss Judy! Look! After a few months in Brazil, my Portuguese was good enough to chat with them.

They were my first Bandeirantes, my Girl Scouts, one of four troops I had recently started as a new Peace Corps volunteer in Brazil. Teenagers with skimpy educations, too many siblings, and dim futures, they had never heard of Girl Scouts until I explained the idea.

In Brazil, scouting was a middle-class luxury. I had had to fight with the local Girl Scout council to start troops in the poor sections of the city. The scouting matrons—as if in uniform themselves, straight hair pulled back into tight, identical buns; nails painted bright red; pearl earrings; and eye makeup cemented in place—had been dubious. They could hardly argue with the avowed ideal that scouting should be for everyone. But poor kids? Dirty kids? In their meetings?

My Bandeirantes had no such doubts. Once I explained scouting, they all wanted to be Girl Scouts. This was something new. What did they have to lose? They never quite understood what the Peace Corps was, either, though they had vaguely heard of Presidente Kennedy, its founder. They just seemed to figure that I was benign and possibly useful, offering something to do besides hanging around Vila Rica in the long afternoons.

To get the uniforms they were so proud of, we had held bake sales and gone door to door begging money from their neighbors, who had given cheerfully whatever they could spare. I then took a few of the girls with me by bus to Americana, a small city about an hour away. At the fabric factory there, we had bought yards of cheap blue material and patterns for the mothers to follow.

To my surprise, the mothers had been as curious as the girls to see what I was up to in their dusty little village. Before starting the troops, I had taken a survey of the women in Vila Rica, a planned village built by the Brazilian housing authority to get rid of the city's notorious favelas—shantytowns with corrugated tin roofs and slapped-together walls.

Going house to house, notebook in hand, I had asked the women seemingly straightforward, innocent questions. The answers stunned me.

"How old are you?" I'd ask a woman, typically a worn-looking soul. They all had that same tired look. Not just not enough sleep the night before, but the type of tired that saps the depths of your being. Their cheeks were hollow, some teeth missing, their hair thinning. Most had a baby at the breast or hip. Their dresses showed the stains of several days' worth of rice and beans. I'd have guessed their ages at forty to fifty.

"Twenty-two," would come the answer. My age.

"How many children do you have?" The woman's forehead would wrinkle, eyes squint.

"What do you mean? Living or dead?"

Dead children? More than one?

"Both," I'd say, dreading the answers: Three dead, six living, said one. Five dead, three living, said another. Four dead, seven living, said a third.

I knew, of course, that Brazil was (and still is) a Catholic country, and that birth control was a taboo subject. I knew I was on shaky ground, as an American, to probe much further. I had heard too often that uneducated Brazilians believed birth control was an American plot designed to reduce Brazil's population to facilitate an American takeover.

Still. I had to do something.

I went to the Johnson & Johnson factory on the outskirts of town and went home with cartons of Kotex and a big poster of the female reproductive system.

A few weeks later, my mouth as hot and dry as the afternoon itself and praying that Vila Rica's resident nun would not stop by, I gathered the girls and their mothers, many of them pregnant or nursing, into the tiny living room of one of the houses.

I put up the poster, pointed to ovaries, fallopian tubes, vagina—a diagram I had known by heart since eighth grade, but something completely foreign to these women. I explained the mechanics—ovulation, menstruation, pregnancy, childbirth.

Puzzled looks. It dawned on me.

"Do you know how a woman gets pregnant?"

More silence. They looked at each other, embarrassed, hushing restless babies.

Of course! I finally got it. When you think about it, the link between sex and conception is actually not obvious. If you have sex all the time and you only get pregnant once a year or so ...

One woman, on the right track, ventured a guess: "Is it when you go to the fields to get water?" Could be. A woman alone in the fields was indeed a ripe target.

I plunged ahead about eggs and sperm, fertile times of the month, less fertile times. Finally, amid excited buzzing, I passed out the free Kotex.

More puzzled looks: "Do we wear these inside or outside our clothes?" Patiently, I explained. Over time, the mothers and I became friends, though despite my persistent efforts to explain biology, they never did grasp how I could be there month after month and never get pregnant myself.

Toward the end of my stay in Brazil, they knew all the Girl Scout songs—including "Vamos, Bandeirantes"—and all the stories by heart. It was time to take them to the citywide scout meeting with all the other troops.

As excited as the first day they had worn their uniforms, they climbed on the bus to town with me, giggling at the bemused stares from the tired passengers riding home from work. At the council meeting, they were shy, but at my urging, eased into the seated circle with the other Girl Scouts. As the leaders called for order so the singing could begin, stage whispers shot 'round the other troops.

"Are these really Girl Scouts? They have no shoes." I glared at the older women, the scout leaders.

My girls began to sing.

It was one of my proudest moments ... and still is.

While I was busy with my Girl Scouts, Bruce decided to join up with some of the other members of our Peace Corps group on a project in the city of Sao Paulo. This meant commuting from Campinas by bus more than an hour each way, but he loved it. The plan, concocted by Sao Paulo city officials, was to build a highway around the city, which meant moving hundreds of the poor people who lived in the shantytowns ("favelas") on top of garbage dumps out to the outskirts of the city.

The Peace Corps men took bricklaying classes and were supposed to teach it to the men from the favelas so those men could build their own new houses out in exurbia and learn a profession while they were at it. The women? If there was a plan for them, I never heard about it. The city's goal was laudably ambitious, but, at least in the short run, anthropologically disastrous. Before the move, the slum dwellers had actually been able to eke out a living by selling paper, cans, bottles, and other detritus from the garbage dump. Once out in the boonies, they were stuck with no way to earn a living. Bricklaying should have been an option, but as Bruce described to me the leaning, wobbly walls the men were building, that did not seem likely.

As our Peace Corps days wound down, I gave birth to our son in the maternity hospital in Campinas. Three months later, we stood on the airport tarmac in Rio de Janeiro. With my baby in my arms, I touched my fingers to my lips, knelt down, and "kissed" the tarmac. I was sure I would get back to Brazil someday. I never have.

But Brazil has never left my heart.

CHAPTER FIVE

Discovering Journalism

On the surface, things seemed okay when we first got back from the Peace Corps. Like everybody else we knew in Cambridge, Massachusetts, we heartily protested the Vietnam War. I cheerfully sang Brazilian drinking songs to our little toddler. We reunited with college friends and ate a lot of pizza.

But maritally, Bruce and I were falling apart, growing ever more distant as we tried to juggle taking care of our son and our grad student lives—the Harvard "ed" school for me, the business school for him. Eventually, the distance between us grew too much. I fell in love with someone else. Though I broke it off and Bruce and I got back together, things were never the same. We struggled on for a couple more years, then agreed on a no-fault divorce. Before our court date, we walked around the Cambridge courthouse holding hands. Neither of us wanted the other to lose contact with our son, so we settled on joint custody—two weeks in my house, two weeks in his. That arrangement seemed fair and enlightened to us at the time, but for a small child, it was terrible. He never really had a place to call home.

As Bruce and I were painfully splitting up, a college friend of his had started working as a reporter at the *Lowell Sun*. In those days, I thought I wanted to be a psychologist and was on a path toward a doctorate. I thought this career choice was simply an intellectual interest in the fascinating world of the human psyche, but I soon realized that studying psychology was an oblique attempt to understand myself and why I was so anxious all the time. Unconsciously, I was ripe for a new idea, and Bruce's friend provided it. "Why not be a reporter?" the friend suggested. He got me an interview at the Lowell paper. I got the job and never looked back.

Like everyone else trying to break into mainstream journalism, I started at the bottom. I put in three years of back-to-back, night-day shifts at the *Sun*, sometimes with walking pneumonia, always with worries about juggling day and night care for my young son. My "beat" was excruciatingly boring—covering the Chelmsford selectmen, who, to a man (and they *were* all men) smoked cigars and wore white bucks and preppy plaid pants.

Eventually, I graduated to the city hall beat in Lowell, trudging down the main street half asleep every morning to see if anything was happening in the tax office and the city manager's office. (Usually, nothing was.) Once a week, I sat through interminable late-night city council meetings where everything had been decided well beforehand behind closed doors. I would rush back to the *Sun* and crank out the news, even if there was none, until one in the morning. Then I'd drive back to Cambridge, relieve the babysitter, and, a few hours later, head back for the eight o'clock shift at the *Sun*.

News droughts notwithstanding, I wrote five or six stories a day in those years, with tense editors ripping the articles from my typewriter (yes, a typewriter, six carbon copies) before I even read them.

It was not clear the editors read them either. My best friend, Celestine, who carpooled with me, was so sure nobody read her stuff that at the end of one story, she typed in the Gettysburg

Address. It ran. The only liberals within miles, she and I were known as the "bra-less babes" from Cambridge, which is to say, it was a fairly unsophisticated newsroom. The court reporter, it was rumored, packed a pearl-handled gun in her purse. A female political reporter, in the indelicate phrase of another colleague, "had her head so far up [a politician]'s ass you can't see her feet."

Still, for someone who had never been allowed to feel, much less speak, the truth growing up, writing the truth was now my job. I even got paid for it, albeit only $89 a week. One of my last articles at the *Sun* was a piece of fiction, a Christmas story. As it turned out, an editor at the *Boston Globe* liked this story so much, he hired me.

SAO PAULO, Brazil—
Christmas is always hot in Sao Paulo.

For the rich, electric fans alleviate the sweltering heat a bit, as do iced gin and tonics.

For Dona Sebastiana, her husband, Joaquim, and their nine children, there was no way to fight the heat, except, of course, by working. It kept the mind off the body's troubles, even at Christmas.

Sebastiana's shack lay close to some twenty other ramshackle "barracas," shacks built from cheap cardboard and stray boards. The group of shacks was not far from one of the major sewage canals in Sao Paulo. The people who lived there had recently been told by the city highway department that their "favela" would be razed to finish a new highway around the outskirts of the city. Even now, on Christmas Day, trucks rumbled along the one open lane of the highway, right next to the shacks.

Most of the shacks were more or less firmly rooted in the large garbage pile that lay along the banks of the canal. Sebastiana worked as a maid, and her husband had managed to acquire a pushcart to sell miniature shish kebabs, but most of the neighbors made their living from the garbage.

They would pick through the garbage for paper that they stuffed into large burlap sacks and carried several miles to paper recycling mills. They sold it to the mills for a pittance, upon which they tried to support their large families. In several days, Christmas wrapping paper dumped in the garbage pile would be a rich source of income for the shack-dwellers.

Even though it was only 5:00 a.m., Dona Sebastiana was sweating when she awoke. Moving quietly so as not to disturb Joaquim and the three children sleeping in their parents' bed, she heated a cup of strong coffee. Sweetening it with four tablespoons of sugar, she gulped it down.

She decided not to have the bread, all that was left from her trip to the store two days before.

"After all, it is Christmas," she mused, "the children need it more than I. I can get a little something later myself."

Dressing herself in cheap Japanese thong sandals, an old, patched, but relatively clean dress, and a scarf tied around her hair, she took 500 cruzeiros from the combination kitchen cabinet and bureau, the only piece of furniture except the table and beds in their tiny home. She stepped out in the already-steaming day.

Joaquim, she knew, would see to it that at least the little ones got some bread and sugar before he went to work at 7:00. Hopefully, Conceicao, the eldest daughter, could watch the baby and the others and wash some of the clothes. Christmas "dinner" would have to be a late afternoon affair.

The bus out to the "American ghetto" was uncrowded at this hour. Sebastiana dozed fitfully throughout the 45-minute ride from her shantytown shack, past the glittering Christmas decorations in downtown, out to the elegant homes in Brooklin.

When she arrived at the back door, she was greeted by the family's two youngest children. The excitement of Christmas had awakened them early. They babbled happily to her in Portuguese and a little English as she got them that strange American breakfast, cereal and milk.

With some slight guilt, Sebastiana assuaged the gnawing growls in her stomach by breaking off a small piece of bread and chewing it quickly. The senhora didn't like maids to eat unless they were specifically offered food. She said that she has had too much trouble with light-fingered maids.

As she shooed the children out into the large back yard so they wouldn't wake their parents too soon, Sebastiana rinsed the rice and washed greens for the salad.

Joaquim by now had also left the shack in the favela, after kissing the children goodbye, wishing them a Merry Christmas, and assuring them he would not work too long this day. The littlest child cried as Joaquim took his push-cart and began walking slowly toward the street that led to the railroad station. Conceicao swept the baby up gently, set him comfortably on her hip, and placed a bit of sweetened bread on his lips.

Joaquim's beat was the main drag in front of the railroad station. He sold his special little shish kebabs made from the guinea pigs he caught by the canal at the favela. Marinated in strong vinegar and oregano and cooked over the small open fire in his pushcart, the meat tasted a little like beef.

At home, Conceicao dressed the little ones and warned them not to go out of the shack. The rats that ran through the garbage night after night had bitten many of the children in the favela lately. The older children pulled on patched shorts and shirts and ran outdoors to find tin cans to play soccer with.

Let the More Loving One Be Me

Absent-mindedly, Conceicao flicked flies off the sleeping baby as she straightened up the shack.

"Christmas," she mused blandly, "it's Christmas." She wanted to do something to surprise her parents when they returned from work, and she wanted to do something for the children, but what? Cook a special dinner? There was some extra rice and twice the quantity of beans they usually had stored in the house. But there was no more sugar for a sweet dessert. There was no milk for the children. There was one small piece of salted meat, which she set in water to soak. It would do no good to run to the neighbors to borrow flour or sugar or margarine. They had nothing either.

In Brooklin, Sebastiana had set the long table with a linen cloth and the family's best silver. The senhora came downstairs in a pretty red dress, looking cool, neat, and festive.

Ashamed of her rags and sandals, Sebastiana wiped her sweaty hands on the back of her dress, as she quietly asked the senhora what she should do next.

With barely a nod of "hello," much less a "Merry Christmas," the senhora told Sebastiana to dress the children, and to do it quickly.

"The guests will be here soon. And, oh, the living room needs to be vacuumed. Hurry, before our friends arrive."

Trying to hurry, but without much energy, Sebastiana rounded up the children and helped them into their fine clothes. The little boy wore starched shorts, embroidered with little animals, and a spanking-clean white shirt complete with his little initials on the collar.

The little girl was dressed like the doll her parents wanted her to be. She wore a petticoat and a pale green sundress. On her feet, she had matching green sandals.

Sebastiana, her thongs slapping quietly on the thick-piled fibers of the carpet, went back downstairs to the vacuum closet. The senhora was there, reaching for the handle of the door at the same moment. The white, manicured hand and slender, but slightly weak forearm, briefly touched Sebastiana's earthy brown and thickly muscled hand.

"I'll get it," muttered Sebastiana.

Relieved that the work was getting done promptly, the senhora quickly withdrew her hand from the unintended contact with Sebastiana. She retired to the kitchen to fix the canapes.

When the guests arrived, Sebastiana slipped into the starched maid's uniform the senhora had provided for the day. Although Sebastiana would stay mostly in the kitchen, she would need to clear plates from the hearty table of 12, and the senhora wanted her dressed appropriately.

The guests threw themselves into the pleasant task of devouring the Christmas bounty—salad, gelatin pates, turkey, ham, two kinds of potatoes, rice, sliced tomatoes, and tiny peas.

A little later, as she scraped the plates, Sebastiana was tempted to take some of the scrapings home to her children. The leftovers alone would feed the family for several days. But if she were caught, she would instantly lose her job and the $3 a day she would earn.

On the other hand, it was Christmas, and why should her children go hungry when the senhora's children had eaten so much that they would vomit before the day was up. To stop her thoughts, Sebastiana moved quickly around the kitchen getting the ingredients for dessert, a baked Alaska.

Quickly but carefully, the senhora helped Sebastiana mold ice cream onto the cake base. Then she spread on the meringue that Sebastiana had whipped by hand. Then quickly into the oven to brown the meringue but not melt the ice cream.

Gracefully, the smiling senhora carried the flaming "piece de resistance" to the dining room and served the dessert with a silver spatula. Each guest received a delicate china plate and a gold dessert fork for the mountainous helping of ice cream.

Peeping through the door, Sebastiana determined that the senhora was completely occupied with her party. The children were skipping around the table, mildly annoying the guests.

Sebastiana quietly closed the door to the dining room. As her fingers reached for a slice of turkey, she thought of her own nine children who had eaten just a swallow of coffee and a small piece of bread. She imagined Conceicao washing the pound of rice and sorting the beans they had left.

Suddenly, Sebastiana choked. She couldn't swallow the meat, starved though her body was for it. Her coughing brought the little girl running in from the dining room.

"Mommy, Mommy!" the little girl skipped out, her voice whining and piercing. "The new maid is eating our food. She can't eat our food."

Flushing but maintaining her social grace, the senhora scolded her daughter for making a fuss.

"Honestly, what can you do with maids?" she said, turning to her closest friend. "I mean, you try to treat them right, and they steal you blind. You can't trust anybody in this country."

Her husband offered cigars around the table, and the group moved slowly into the living room. A guest sat down at the brocaded piano stool and began to play Christmas carols. Sipping after-dinner liqueurs, the guests gathered round to sing carols, drunkenly.

After a while, the senhora slipped away to find Sebastiana.

When Sebastiana heard the little girl tattling about the

piece of meat, she whispered an oath under her breath. It was all the anger she could manage. Hunger and discouragement make anger a waste of precious energy.

If she stole meat for her children, she would certainly lose her job. But that would be later. The family was hungry today.

"I, too, am hungry," she thought.

Another peek through a crack in the door assured her that she had several minutes before the impending scene with the senhora. She quickly slipped out of her maid's uniform and hung it neatly on the hook behind the maid's room door.

Comfortable once again in her own dress and thong sandals, she fumbled through the kitchen cabinets for a bag.

Decisive now, she took the scrapings that she had put in the plastic garbage bag and stuffed them into her own bag. She did not touch the part of the turkey that was still uncarved, nor did she take the unserved salad greens or boiled potatoes.

She took from the dinner plates the bits of meat, covered with gravy that the well-fed guests could not consume. It formed one soupy pile in the plastic bag. When all twelve plates were scraped clean, she peeked again through the door.

The senhora was coming.

Grabbing the plastic bag in her left hand, Sebastiana started for the back door. On the counter by the door was a small truck that the little boy had played with and then forgotten. Quickly, Sebastiana grabbed it and stuffed it into the top of her dress.

She was out the door and past the driveway when she heard the back door slam.

"The senhora is angry. She will have all those dishes to do by herself now," thought Sebastiana, allowing herself a fleeting smile at the idea.

Let the More Loving One Be Me

At the edge of the driveway, the senhora stood with her hands on her hips, sweat breaking out on her forehead. She wanted to yell at Sebastiana, but that would create a scene.

"Americans hate scenes," thought Sebastiana as she hurriedly turned the corner to escape the senhora's stare.

As she approached the bus stop, it dawned on Sebastiana that the bus would do her no good. She had not been paid today, and she did not have the 500 cruzeiros for the ride. The 45-minute bus ride was a good three hours' walk, and by now, it was afternoon, easily 95 degrees.

Hurrying was impossible because of the heat, so Sebastiana walked slowly but steadily, keeping on the shady side of the street whenever she could.

Feeling little guilt, she thought only of the food she had in the plastic bag. It didn't bother her that she had stolen garbage. It was food. She hadn't planned to steal it. It had just happened.

The sun was still hot as she approached her shantytown. She could see Joaquim's pushcart in front of the shack. Quickening her step in anticipation of being with her family again, she shuffled to the house.

On the table, she immediately saw two large loaves of bread and a small tray of coconut cookies. She knew the money Joaquim made from selling his shish kebabs would never have paid for all of that.

As he rolled a homemade cigarette, Joaquim looked at his wife. She set her plastic bag on the table. They said nothing, and their eyes barely smiled. She did not ask him where the bread and sweets came from, and he did not ask about the food she brought.

The children saw the food on the table and jumped and laughed and pulled at Sebastian's skirt.

"It's Christmas, it's Christmas!" They laughed as they swarmed around her. "Let's have a party!" Conceicao took charge. She put chairs at the table for her parents and then seated the children so that they could share the few plates.

"Eat it slowly, children," said Joaquim.

Sebastiana took a drag from Joaquim's cigarette and nibbled at her food while the children ate. After the meal, Sebastiana pulled the truck from her dress and gave it to the baby. The baby's little fist clutched the shiny toy and would not give it up.

The older children looked on at the baby's oblivious happiness, not asking if there were presents for them. They then went outside for more soccer and joking around, happy now and temporarily well-fed.

"Come sit by me," said Joaquim. Sebastiana drew her chair close to his by the door. There was a slight breeze, but not enough to keep the flies away from the baby.

Christmas is always hot in Sao Paulo.

From my first days and nights in a newsroom, my curiosity and my growing passion for digging out the truth steadily propelled me. In the early days, when Associated Press news from around the world would be spit out in long paper scrolls from printer machines in the corner of the newsroom, I would stand there for minutes on end, watching, reading, marveling that I, a newbie to the profession, was able to watch all this news just pouring in, story after story, exciting stories, disasters, politics, the entire globe spinning out in front of me. *If I have to die,* I remember thinking, *I want to die right here in a newsroom, smack in the middle of things.*

And, right from the start, I became a fervent pursuer of the truth, wherever it led me, not just because I was motivated to understand the truth of the family I grew up in, but also to understand the wider world and the importance of telling the truth for the sake of democracy. I became a passionate defender of the freedom of the press in general and the First Amendment in particular.

On the wall in my study hangs a framed cover of the *New Yorker* from January 19, 2015.

The picture shows the magnificent Eiffel Tower in Paris, surrounded, at the bottom, by fiery red foliage. The upper part of the image shows, instead of the actual graceful tower itself, a long, sharpened pencil, a symbol of the power of the press and a monument to the French satirical weekly *Charlie Hebdo*.

Twelve days earlier, two French Muslim brothers, members of Al-Qaeda in the Arabian Peninsula, had barged into the magazine's offices, killed twelve people, and injured eleven others in protest against the magazine, which had run cartoons mocking the Islamic Prophet Muhammad. (The magazine had also lampooned Catholicism and Judaism.)

Somehow, the surviving staff members of *Charlie Hebdo* managed to keep going. The next issue featured a cover cartoon of a Muslim prophet holding a sign that read Je Suis Charlie ("I am Charlie," an emphatic affirmation of freedom of the press). The print run was almost eight million copies in six languages, compared to its usual run of sixty thousand, only in French. A much-needed victory for the free press.

On the bookshelf in my study is one of the most important books I have ever read, *Freedom for the Thought That We Hate*, by the late Anthony Lewis, the two-time Pulitzer Prize–winning columnist for the *New York Times*.

Lewis's title comes directly from the late Supreme Court Justice Oliver Wendell Holmes Jr. In an opinion he wrote in 1929, Holmes wrote that a constitutional imperative is the "principle of free thought—not free thought for those who agree with us but freedom for the thought that we hate."

Amen.

And oh shit.

I have always been drawn to one particular incident. In 1977, the village of Skokie, near Chicago, had a large Jewish population, many of whom were survivors of Nazi concentration camps. An American Nazi group was planning a demonstration in Skokie, complete with Nazi demonstrators holding swastikas. Horrified, the village authorities passed ordinances banning the dissemination of signs and clothing that advocated hatred against certain people. Lawsuits ensued, eventually making their way to the US Court of Appeals, which thankfully and agonizingly ruled that these ordinances were unconstitutional. An excruciating decision, but absolutely necessary protection for the thought we hate.

A more personal experience of the emotional struggle involved in allowing the freedom to speak and write hateful thoughts was the intense inner conflict I felt when radical feminists were trying to ban pornography because of its potentially dangerous effects on women. It was the late '70s, or early '80s, and I was a young reporter for the *Boston Globe*.

I was covering an anti-pornography rally featuring the late Andrea Dworkin, a radical feminist. Her deep rage and disheveled appearance were difficult to be around. Yet the feminist in me was riveted by the power of her anger, the fervor of her commitment to protect women, and her insistence that the principle of free speech should not be used to protect porn, which often featured images of women being sexually abused and assaulted. Those images had the potential to promote further abuse of women, she argued. At the time, I hadn't yet acknowledged to myself my father's sexual abuse.

As I struggled to write my story fairly, the feminist in me waged an all-out battle against the journalist in me. By deadline, the free-speech journalist had won. Barely. Another agonizing victory for freedom for the thought we hate.

Short of speech that incites imminent, lawless action (the US Supreme Court's 1969 so-called Brandenburg test), I am close to a free-speech absolutist. I strongly believe it is more dangerous for governments to suppress speech, including horrible, insulting, degrading, offensive speech, than for such speech to be spoken, printed, or videotaped.

But it's hard, so very hard. I have had to write stories trying to be fair to antiabortionists, despite my outrage at the idea that someone else's religious belief could control my body.

I have had to give space and ink to creationists whose ignorance of, and hostility to, evolution drove me nuts. I have had to accurately quote gun rights activists even as my anti-gun guts churned.

And it's not just hate speech that is tricky. It's that the truth, or truths, can be hard to find amid all the noise.

The journalistic tendency for handling controversy is often the "he said, she said" approach, as if the truth were fifty-fifty. But in reality, truth does not have equal sides.

Data matters. Facts matter. Science matters. The earth is not flat. Some people are actually right and some wrong. Lies are lies no matter who says them or who sits in the Oval Office. Sometimes the emperor really has no clothes. And it's a journalist's job to say so. That's what makes journalism the essential and challenging profession that it is.

I thrived right from the first at the *Globe*. Everybody did. In my early days there, it was edited by Tom Winship, who helped the *Globe* get the Pentagon Papers and sent out frequent "tiger notes": ("Great job, kid!"). Indeed, he seemed to have as much fun running the *Globe* as the rest of us did writing it. *The Globe* was a happy place. Over time, the newsroom culture and editors changed, especially after the paper was bought by the *New York Times* in 1993. But I always loved working there. In fact, one of my earliest reporting forays at the *Globe* is still one of my favorites.

Discovering Journalism

‍ঌ

She was a dainty sprite of a child, just six years old back then in 1981, tumbling like a pro on the backyard trampoline in Cambridge, straight black hair swinging hard as she bounced, legs strong and shapely, skin a rich brown.

"She shouldn't even be alive," her blonde, blue-eyed mother, Pam, murmured to me. "We got her out of Cambodia just before it collapsed. Her plane was being shelled when it took off."

I stood in awe in that sunny backyard. The *Globe* had sent me to interview Pam and her husband for a story on the newly booming business of foreign adoptions. They had adopted six children from foreign countries and had three biological kids of their own.

Nearly 5,000 foreign children a year were being adopted by Americans because there weren't enough American babies to go around. In baby-rich developing countries like Cambodia and Vietnam, adults were victims of war, poverty, or excess fertility. Their kids wound up in the streets or orphanages.

In baby-poor countries like the US, desperate would-be parents, many with infertility, were waiting as long as eight years to adopt infants and children. Better birth control, better access to abortion, and more unwed women keeping their babies had wiped out America's supply of adoptable babies.

None of which interested me at the moment.

I was mesmerized by Siri, bouncing joyfully as her mother recounted her story.

Siri had been found crying on a road in Cambodia, an unimaginably tiny human being weighing only two pounds. She was so small that she was carried in a pocketbook to an orphanage, where the nuns nicknamed her the "pocketbook baby."

A memory tugged. Pocketbook baby, pocketbook baby. Suddenly, I knew.

This must be the little girl the *Globe* had written about six years earlier, during the frantic "baby-lift" while Saigon was falling. The story had been written by Matt Storin, now the *Globe*'s editor, but at the time, the paper's Asia bureau chief. His story had been heartbreaking. No one could read it and think this tiny child would survive.

Rushing back to the *Globe*, I parked crookedly, didn't stop to put my purse on my desk, and all but ran to the corner office where Matt sat hunched over his computer.

He looked up, a hint of irritation flickering across his face. Most reporters didn't barge into his office. He was a straight news guy, no fluff. He did not suffer fools gladly. Or at all.

"Matt, can I talk to you for a second?" I ventured.

"What's up?" His eyes flicked to me, then back to his keyboard.

"Do you remember the story you did about the pocketbook baby?"

He went still, looked straight at me.

"What." More a flat statement than a question.

"She's alive. She's in Cambridge, doing flips on a trampoline. She's six years old. She was adopted by a Cambridge couple. She looks fantastic."

Matt sank back in his chair, his body soft, his eyes misty.

"Write it," he said. "Extra space if you need it."

I turned to go.

"Hey, thanks. Thanks for telling me."

I went back to my desk and, through my own tears, wrote the story. Matt put it on Page One.

Though the *Globe* was, and still is, one of the country's best newspapers, we were allowed, every once in a long while, some moments of levity. With that spirit in mind, I felt free to take a chance one otherwise gloomy day in March 1982.

I had been sent to Cambridge, where workers on the Red Line branch of the subway, which was being extended from Harvard Square to Porter Square, had managed to flood a cozy kids' bookstore. After surveying the damage and interviewing the construction company and the bookstore owner, I drove back to the *Globe*, silently chanting the delightfully rhythmic name of the construction company: Morrison-Knudsen, White Mergentime. No doubt about it, my story had to be a poem. Without telegraphing my intent, I sat down and, with an hour or so until deadline, began to type.

Poetic Justice

'Twas the night after Christmas in '79,
Thomas Murray—the bookman—discovered the slime.
It had dripped. It had sprayed. It had poured through
    the night,
And it drowned his best books! Consider his plight!
For a year plus two months, he had happily run
Small World of Books, a kids' store that was fun.
To Mass Ave in Cambridge, the kids dragged their folks
To hear stories, watch jugglers, and listen to jokes.
On that night after Christmas, he heard water
    whooshing,"
Ran down to the basement, pulling and pushing,
His 3,000 books were all covered in muck
And the kids, like Tom Murray, were plumb out of luck.
Now Murray is lanky and talky and tall
But when his books drowned, he felt overly small.
He knew nothing of lawyers, the growing Red Line
Nor of Morrison-Knudsen, White Mergentime.
For six months, he sought to find out who was who
And who was to blame for all of the goo.
With no books to sell, Murray's credit was "shot."
His publishers spurned him. His cash flow was not.
Now Morrison-Knudsen, White Mergentime
Were busy constructing the brand-new Red Line
When sixty feet down, they'd got up to the hilt

Let the More Loving One Be Me

In ton upon ton of wet, sandy silt.
In theory, at least, all the water and silt
Were pumped to the street where a big tank was built.
The gunk was supposed to have stayed in the tank
And the water, to go to the sewer, so dank.
But the silt hit the sewer that fateful December,
Clogged everything up, a night to remember!
In the flash of the flood on that night and the next
Murray lost half his stock. Small World was hexed.
Eighty-six thousand dollars, he'd earned for that year;
But without all his books, he was out on his ear.
Two years after the mess—a very bad break—
Thirty-three thousand dollars was all he could make.
So Murray decided to spend his last dime
Fighting Morrison-Knudsen, White Mergentime.
He succeeded at last in reversing the hex
In the courthouse, last week, of old Middlesex.
The jury, consisting of twelve of his peers,
Sent Morrison-Knudsen out on their rears.
Eighty-three thousand dollars, Murray's lawyer
        had said,
For damage, lost profits, and good credit, dead.
No way, said the jury, we're little guys too.
Eighty-seven thousand dollars is your rightful due.
The MBTA's partly caused your bad time.
But mostly, it's Morrison-Knudsen, White Mergentime.
For Small World of Books, this story's not done.
From Morrison-Knudsen, the word is still mum.
But the MBTA has let leak, with a squeal
That their side—and MK—may soon file an appeal.

In the wonderful spirit of the *Globe* in those days, my editors caught the lightheartedness of the poem. They headlined my story "Poetic justice in the first round: Wherein a solitary book-man triumphs over corporation, government, and nature." And they added an "editor's note:"

> In the spirit of telling our readers this tale
> 'bout a man who told stories and had books for sale,
> We have opted to give you the facts all in verse
> Like stories for children as read by a nurse.

Most of my stories at the *Globe*, of course, were less lighthearted, pure facts, and little to no editorializing. Opinions and feelings were the domain of columnists and the editorial page writers, thanks to what we called the strict separation of "church" (the editorial page) and "state" (the newsroom). The total opposite of Fox News today. But an experience I had going around in a wheelchair for a day was one of the exceptions and was hard to process precisely because it did involve allowing feelings, so forbidden in my family, to show.

I hung up the phone, wondering what, exactly, I had just agreed to.

Stuffing my feet into my sandals, I walked to the *Boston Globe* city desk and caught my editor's eye. He held up a "one sec" finger, wound up his call and turned to me.

"What's up, kid?" he asked. At 40, Jon was only 5 years my senior.

I took a breath. "I just told a guy named Marc, the new deputy director of the state office of handicapped affairs, that I'd go around with him in a wheelchair for a day. This afternoon, actually. At the State House. He wants me to show readers the barriers that still exist for people in wheelchairs."

"Great idea! First person story. I'll do the photo order," he said, typing it up.

"I was kind of hoping you'd say no. The 'No First Person' rule and all...."

Let the More Loving One Be Me

"Go."

I drove to the Brookline address Marc had given me. I rang his bell. He must have pressed some button. The door opened. "My" wheelchair sat waiting, taunting, two huge wheels in back, two small ones in front. I stared at it, then remembered my manners. I stuck out my right hand to greet the handsome young man waiting for me. Could he shake my hand? He was paralyzed, having broken his neck four years earlier in a car crash. He used to swim for Harvard. His trophies sat on his bookshelf. In the team picture, he was one of the biggest, a good 200 pounds with huge shoulders, a torso that tapered nicely to slim hips. He extended his right hand. His fingers didn't really work. We shook, sort of.

"Marc." He smiled pleasantly. He was 24, with black hair, glasses and a bushy mustache, a little pale, but dressed neatly in a business suit and colorful tie, not slumping in his chair. One hundred forty pounds max. I wondered how long it had taken him to get dressed.

I glanced at the wheelchair and promptly sat on the couch.

"Before we get into the van," I said, "I should run down to my car and roll up the windows." I froze. People with disabilities don't run.

"Oops, sorry," I managed, feeling the heat rise up my neck.

"No worries, Judy. I used to run around myself."

"How did you ever get used to not being able to?" I didn't even have my notebook out yet, but this had suddenly become more than just a story. I had to know.

"You don't," he said. "In my dreams, I still walk and run."

"And when you wake up?"

"I manage. It's better than being dead. That was the other so-called option."

I made a quick trip down to roll up my car windows. Back in Marc's apartment, I went over to the wheelchair, plumped up the foam cushion and finally, sat. I immediately felt awkward, and I hadn't even tried to move it. The seat was hard against my legs. I smiled at Marc: "Let's go."

Steering was not so bad, sort of like turning a canoe by moving one wheel backward and the other forward. But the wheels kept sticking out farther than I thought. I banged into the doorway. Marc followed me into the hallway. I got to the elevator first.

At the elevator, I couldn't reach the button. Marc, using a kind of throwing motion to bang his knuckle against the button, succeeded.

I started in first.

"Can you manage by yourself? It will only fit one of us," said Marc.

Inside, I was faced all wrong, with my back to the door. Twisting around, I sat through the ride with my finger lightly on the Door Open button, afraid of getting stuck when the door opened. I made it, wheeling out backward.

"I can do this!" I thought. Then it hit me. My world had shrunk so much already that in just five minutes, negotiating a lousy elevator had become a big deal.

Outside, Marc showed me how to get onto the mechanized ramp to the van. But I forgot to lock my wheels and started to slide down. The driver-attendant rushed over and locked them for me.

Inside the van, I banged my elbow trying to back into my place along the van wall. I got my small wheels, which kept going their own way, tangled with Marc's.

Marc ripped off two MBTA tickets from his booklet using his hands and his teeth. I looked away. Out the window, I saw a woman bicycling and a man jogging and couldn't help thinking, "Freedom!"

"Don't you envy those people outside, running and biking?" I asked.

"Of course. But one doc told me right after the accident that within a year, I'd have the emotional maturity of a 50-year-old. Change what you can. Accept what you can't." Wise old words from such a young man.

I was an athlete, but I couldn't even wheel myself up the twisty ramp to the McCormick building at the State House. Embarrassed, enraged, I was a baby in a carriage. The van driver wheeled me up. Marc wheeled himself up.

Then, a revolving door. Who built the world this way? Marc spotted a side door. It was only marginally better, though. With its round doorknob, Marc could not really grip the handle, but using gravity and the weight of his hand, he opened the door and wheeled through.

I couldn't. I couldn't reach far enough out from my sitting position to push the door with one hand and move my wheelchair forward with the other. Wheeling with only one wheel turned the chair. My foot pedals clanged into the doorjamb. Finally, some kind soul held the door for me. I was beginning to be on the lookout for kind souls wherever they might be amid the multitudes rushing around.

"If they put levers on these doors instead of doorknobs, people with disabilities could open them. So could people carrying bundles," said Marc matter-of-factly.

I needed to use the ladies' room. I was blocked by a huge, heavy door with yet another round doorknob. A man, another kind soul, held it open for me. Inside, two stalls. I aimed for the closer one. My chair wouldn't fit, so I transferred my weight, one hand on the none-too-sturdy toilet paper dispenser and the other on the seat. The bottom of my skirt dipped into the water and got soaked.

Out in the hallway again, I realized I was getting used to endless physical obstacles. "Okay, I'm disabled," I thought. "This is my life. If Marc can manage, so can I."

Or could I?

As the physical barriers became more familiar, more subtle ones intruded. A good-looking man in a three-piece suit attracted my attention. Normally, there would be eye contact, the flicker of a smile. Today, nothing. I was invisible.

In the afternoon, Marc and I wheeled ourselves into a conference room to meet with a group of high school kids in wheelchairs. Something seemed wrong. The kids looked and acted odd, maybe mentally ill, maybe cognitively impaired. Some of their heads drooped, some hands jerked.

Panic. I usually thought of myself as tolerant, open, respectful, but all I could think was, "Don't let anybody see me with them."

I realized that this was the lesson I would carry with me for the rest of my life, this odd hierarchy of stigma. Again, I was appalled by my own prejudices.

Marc wheeled up to me. This day, which I once thought would never end, was about to. I had survived, albeit humbled, and in awe of Marc and the millions like him whose wheelchairs are forever, not just one day.

As I sat there, an old janitor with white hair paused on his rounds. "It's amazing how you people get around," he said.

He was the only person all day who actually stopped to talk.

To me, the *Globe* newsroom felt like a little village. Unlike my family, it was a place where I felt safe and secure. I was seen and heard. I had a clear role. Most of all, I belonged, a new and wonderful feeling. The newsroom underwent a number of renovations and shuffling of desks, but eventually, I ended up with a desk near the door to the parking lot. It was a lucky spot. It gave me the opportunity to see people sneaking out early and to watch the guys (it was always the guys) heading out to play basketball at lunchtime at nearby UMass Boston, while the women held the fort.

Our desks were close together, maybe four or five feet apart, so there was zero privacy. I loved it. Many afternoons as deadline approached, I'd overhear my closest neighbor, Scott, take a call from his very young daughter, who had somehow learned the mechanics of speed dial. He'd stop his frantic typing, sit back a moment, listen with a smile on his face, then say, "I have to go now, sweetie. Can you put Mom on?"

Another close neighbor, Dick, like me, a medical writer, sat behind so many stacks of papers and books that it was easier to hear than to see him. That proved useful for evading wandering editors. Eavesdropping on my other nearby neighbor, David, also buried in stuff, I learned more about space and physics than I ever had in school. Across the aisle, the business writers whooped it up whenever big things happened, like the Dow hitting 10,000 for the first time. (This was, admittedly, quite a while ago.)

On days when something really big happened in the world, the newsroom reacted vigorously. On one unforgettable day in 1995, we all stopped work and jumped up from our desks to gather in front of the TVs scattered around the newsroom. The so-called dream team of lawyers had just managed to convince a jury to acquit football star O. J. Simpson of the murders of his ex-wife and her friend after a long, spellbinding trial. The white reporters and editors stood in shocked disbelief that this obvious murderer had gotten off. The Black reporters, fewer in number, were also quiet, but seemed, at least to me, to feel a sense of relief that, for once, a jury had not convicted a Black man.

We had had our own *Globe* dream team, too, which I was lucky enough to be a part of.

It was a beautiful Sunday afternoon, May 2, 1993. I was in the backyard, up to my elbows in weeds, trimming bushes. While my gloves protected my hands, my forearms were another story. They were scratched and made an angry red by the more aggressive plants thriving in Cambridge that spring.

Upstairs, the kitchen phone rang, audible through the sliding glass door that opened onto our second-floor deck. Tossing gloves and pruning shears to the dirt, I ran up the stairs.

"Hello?"

"Hi, Judy." I recognized the voice of a doctor friend, one of Boston's most prominent cardiologists and a person whom, as a *Globe* medical writer, I thoroughly trusted. "Can we go off the record? It's about Reggie Lewis."

"Reggie Who?"

"Reggie Lewis. Captain of the Celtics. The guy who collapsed last week during a game. He's at the Baptist. He has cardiomyopathy."

"Never heard of him. He has what?"

Discovering Journalism

I grabbed a piece of paper and began scribbling, all thoughts of the garden lost. Reggie Lewis, a tall, handsome guy who was head of what fans called the Celtics' Dream Team, had scored ten points against Charlotte in the first three minutes of last Thursday's game, then stumbled and collapsed while running down the court. Video tapes showed that he hadn't been shoved or even touched. He just crashed on his own, face first.

I followed the Red Sox, sort of. But the only thing I knew about the Celtics was how to pronounce the name the Boston way, not the Gaelic way.

I began firing off questions, every so often prying my sweaty arm off the paper, my notes wandering, with arrows, all over the page. What's cardiomyopathy? Damage to heart tissue that can cause the heart to beat irregularly. OK. Is it fatal? Yes, often. What causes it, drugs? Can be. Like cocaine? Yes, among other things. Can I call you back in ten minutes?

I grabbed a glass of water, sat down at my desk, and called the City Desk.

A college kid, an intern, was on duty.

"I just got a call from a cardiologist about a basketball player named Reggie Lewis. He has some kind of heart damage. Twelve cardiologists apparently just examined him. He's at New England Baptist Hospital. Is this important?"

"Holy shit," the young voice said. "Hang on."

The editor picked up. "What do you have on Reggie Lewis?" I told him.

"I'll hook you up with Steve."

"Steve who?" I never read the sports pages.

"The sportswriter. Double byline. Page One. You have one hour."

Sunday night dinner went the way of the gardening.

Apparently, I had the scoop of the year, a scoop I couldn't have imagined would lead to both glory and humiliation.

Steve and I collaborated on a Page One story for the next day. A dream team of doctors, the twelve biggest names in Boston cardiology, had been secretly convened by the basketball team's physician, Dr. Arnold Scheller, to meet at New England Baptist Hospital, where Lewis had been hospitalized following his collapse.

The diagnosis, as my source had told me, was not promising—cardiomyopathy. With this life-threatening condition, Reggie, a hero to the whole city (except, apparently, to me) would probably never play again.

At the *Globe*, the "glass houses," as we called the top brass who worked in the glass-walled offices around the edge of the newsroom, conferred. The *Globe* would have its own so-called dream team. It would consist of Steve, the sportswriter; Jackie, another sportswriter; Dan, a dazzlingly good general reporter; another Steve, a multiple-Pulitzer Prize winner; Howard, a feature writer; and me.

The official goal was to find out what ailed Reggie Lewis and whether Boston's hero had taken cocaine. The other, unstated but always understood, goal was to get a Pulitzer. The story had everything—sports, medicine, drugs, and race, because Reggie was Black. All we needed was the smoking gun—proof that Reggie had used cocaine.

In a surprise move that stunned the city—and us—Lewis fled the Baptist under cover of darkness the night after our first story. He left by truck, not ambulance, leaving behind the wisdom of the medical team. Pissed off that the famous doctors had not included her in their discussions, Lewis's wife, Donna Harris-Lewis, had engineered the late-night move to Brigham and Women's Hospital. Nobody was happy.

Lewis became the responsibility of Dr. Gilbert Mudge, a prominent cardiologist, though not part of the Baptist team. It was, as it turned out, a fateful choice for Lewis.

Inside the *Globe*, pressure from the glass houses was intense, rippling palpably through the newsroom. This was becoming a national story. We had to be first, and we had to be right. Things were moving fast.

Five days after our first story, Jackie, the sportswriter, got a tip from one of her sources. Almost simultaneously, I got a tip from one of mine: Reggie Lewis was set to have surgery very soon to have a defibrillator implanted—a device that could quickly restore an erratic heart rhythm to normal.

The operating room had been booked, her source said. Mine wasn't sure but also thought it might have been. Reggie might play again after all, though one of my sources said on the record, that even with a defibrillator, it "would be crazy" to play pro ball with cardiomyopathy.

Our editors were ecstatic. Another exclusive. Jackie and I wrote the story. It ran, Page One. Boston went wild. The mighty hero might come back. We were the stars now.

Then, chaos. Off-the-record calls began coming in. There would be no surgery. Our story was wrong. It had probably been transiently true. But it didn't stay true.

I had half an hour to write a Page One retraction for the next day. Humiliation kept me awake all that night. But the worst was yet to come.

Two days later, Dr. Mudge called a press conference at the Brigham. Mudge's wife sat in the row ahead of me. She turned around to glare.

"You got it totally wrong," she hissed. "You should be ashamed."

I tried to stare boldly back. What on earth was happening? I wanted to sink through the floor.

Mudge strode confidently to the podium, looked around the packed press room, and let his smug eyes linger on mine.

Reggie Lewis has "neurocardiogenic syncope," he announced.

I panicked. "What the hell is that?" I wondered. I couldn't even spell it.

Neurocardiogenic syncope was, Mudge explained, a benign fainting condition. In a confident manner and equally confident language, he said Lewis showed no signs of cardiomyopathy and no abnormal life-threatening arrhythmias. Reggie could play again.

Were all of my sources wrong? Was the medical dream team crazy? Had I totally screwed up? Again? I drove back to the *Globe*, panicked and feeling sick to my stomach.

In a frenzy, I called my medical dream team sources. They were starting to clam up, under increasing pressure from hospital public relations departments who wanted nothing more than to get their docs out of the fray and out of the headlines. Secret phone calls ensued as a few brave souls stood by my reporting and their original diagnosis. I put their skeptical comments about Mudge's diagnosis in my story. The pace slowed. Day after day, as the summer chugged on, we pursued our sources. We met repeatedly with Mudge, who wouldn't say whether Reggie had used cocaine, though we were pretty sure he knew.

We met with other doctors, who taught me more about cardiomyopathy than I ever wanted to know. Howard, the Black reporter on our team, set out, as he put it, to do "the brother thing," schmoozing with Reggie Lewis's teammates, family, and friends, looking for anyone with solid evidence—as opposed to the rumors we kept hearing—that Reggie had used cocaine.

Meanwhile, under Mudge's guidance, Reggie went back to shooting baskets, training at Brandeis. On July 27, during one of those practices, Reggie Lewis dropped dead. Sudden cardiac death. Just what the medical dream team had predicted.

For the next eleven years, Lewis's wife, Donna Harris-Lewis, pursued Mudge in court, alleging that his negligence had caused Reggie's death. The first trial ended with the jury deadlocked, resulting in a mistrial. The second trial found that Mudge was not to blame for Lewis's death. Donna Harris-Lewis tried for a third trial in 2004 and failed.

And the *Globe* dream team?

We kept reporting the Reggie story all through that endless summer. Our suspicions never went away, but we could not prove that Reggie had used cocaine. We wrote a long story in September, without that smoking gun. No Pulitzer.

But collectively, we did get an award, the Associated Press Sports Editors first place award for Best Investigative Reporting, my first and only prize for sportswriting. Whoop-di-doo.

CHAPTER SIX

Discovering Love, Again

As my professional life thrived, my personal life remained a mess. I loved being a mom. I loved singing to my son and reading to him, and as he grew, I loved watching him come home from school with his two buddies. I still didn't have much money, but my grandmother had given me a few thousand dollars, and we lived in a fairly nice neighborhood in Cambridge. Remarkably, this small sum was enough to put a down payment on a two-family house, thanks to substantial help from my then-boyfriend. It was a great, albeit basic, home.

I loved that my son and two of his friends used to make the rounds, eating their way through all three houses. In the evenings, I often sat on the front porch, chatting with neighbors and watching our community life unfold. I knew who was sick, who had just had a baby, who was dating someone new. On Sunday afternoons, we would gather in one or another backyard, collectively doing the *New York Times* crossword puzzle, and often bringing our voices, guitars, and improvised drums for jam sessions. My specialty was playing the spoons.

Still, I was desperately lonely. Match.com hadn't been invented yet. I went to endless parties, but all the men were married. I was attracted to a few guys at the *Globe*, but nothing panned out, and I didn't really want to mix love and work anyway. I had a seven-year on-again, off-again romance with a very nice man, but I was never really happy with him and eventually managed to break if off for good.

Finally, it dawned on me that if I was serious about meeting someone, I had to go where the men were, and go without the crutch of a female friend. I joined the Appalachian Mountain Club and went on hiking weekends, though I hated hiking in New England. If it wasn't cold and dreary, it was hot and buggy. Uphill was hard, and downhill was even harder on the knees. But one wintry weekend, I screwed up my courage and took myself to Cardigan Lodge in Alexandria, New Hampshire, for a weekend of cross-country skiing, which I did like, and folk dancing, which I liked even better.

After one dance, the tall, bespectacled guy I'd been dancing with kept hold of my hand when the dance was over. Wow. Something was happening. We danced the next dance. And the next one. We talked. His name was Tom. He was a laser physicist. He was fifty-two. He'd never been married. And he lived almost right around the corner from me in Cambridge. Later that night, up in the women's bunk room, I couldn't stop talking about him. A fifty-two-year-old, never-married physicist? Why hadn't he married? Weren't physicists all numbers guys, no feelings? It didn't seem promising. But I liked him. "Go for it," one of my bunk mates urged.

I did.

Tom and I quickly became an item, aided significantly by the fact that we lived so close to each other. He was in no rush to live together or—yikes!—get married. But I was. By this time, my son was a teenager, and Tom, aside from his other reservations, was not keen on living with a teenager. Nor was my son eager to have another father. He already had one, he made very clear to me, and one was enough.

"But I want the three of us to be a real family," I moaned to the therapist I had begun seeing.

The therapist shook his head.

"Don't push it. You'll drive them both away." Luckily, I listened, and the three of us got along just fine.

Tom's house, like mine, was a two-family. He agreed to kick out his upstairs tenant, poor woman, and my son and I moved into that unit. Tom installed a door, which he could lock, between the units. He was worried that my son might mess with his hi-fi, his physics journals, his books. That wouldn't have happened, and didn't, of course, but Tom couldn't have known that in advance.

Tom and I had twenty-two years together, living together by turning the upstairs and downstairs into a more or less coherent whole after my son went off to college. We began seeing a therapist together to discuss marriage. I was ready, Tom said he was not, though secretly, I thought he was. I argued, "If not now, when?" A good point, apparently. He proposed. We got married in a lovely setting at my beloved Wellesley College, our families cheering us on.

I not only loved Tom but felt immensely grateful. He made me a happily married woman. He could never understand the family I grew up in—nor did I yet, for that matter. I still hadn't acknowledged the depth of my childhood trauma, much less connected that to my frequent anxiety. But Tom understood his own trauma all too well.

He had been born in Vienna to Jewish parents. When Tom was about five, the Nazis were threatening. Just ahead of the Anschluss in 1938, Tom, his baby sister, and his parents fled, tearfully leaving behind his grandmother, who couldn't get a visa and ended up dying in the Theresienstadt concentration camp.

Tom lived with that sadness all his life. He had flashbacks. If his car got towed, he was desperate—how could he escape if he had to? After all, his family had barely escaped. Over the years, he became a sophisticated world traveler, not just for adventure, but for a sense of mastery, a glimpse of what a safe world could finally feel like. He was always a bit surprised, though, not to mention relieved, to come home and find his house still there. Tom's experience made me exquisitely sensitive to anti-Semitism and the Holocaust. A column I wrote about the Holocaust sticks with me to this day.

A Healing Hope

In the Lodz ghetto in Poland, home to as many as 204,000 Jews during World War II, there were 170 doctors, as well as a few nurses and midwives, according to numerous diaries and memoirs.

Like all the others, the Jewish healers lived with the daily terror of being shipped off to a death camp. Still, they tended to their fellow inmates, providing care when they could, solace when they couldn't.

There was almost no food, no medication, and certainly no X-ray machines, laboratories, or any of the other accoutrements that we think of as essential to medicine today.

And yet, when there was nothing to give the sick, the Lodz doctors did find something.

"These doctors gave people hope," said Dr. Harold Bursztajn, a Beth Israel Deaconess Medical Center psychiatrist whose parents lived in the ghetto and who spoke about the Lodz experience at a recent meeting for colleagues.

The lesson for today's doctors, who are often demoralized and squeezed ever more tightly by time and budget constraints, is that even "under the most extreme circumstances, in the face of isolation, helplessness, and hopelessness . . . even when there are no medicines, you can use yourself," he said. "The doctor becomes the medicine."

Ghetto doctors, armed with little more than kindness

and hope, twice saved the life of Bursztajn's father, Abraham. The first time, said Bursztajn, was when his father fainted after being tortured. A ghetto doctor revived him.

"I will die here," his despairing father had said to the doctor, an older man.

"One of us will, but it will be me," the physician answered. "I do not have any way to treat you, but you are young. If you don't give up hope, you will survive."

Thanks to that doctor, his father did maintain hope, Bursztajn said, and that hope fueled his courage to resist.

One night, Abraham sneaked out of the ghetto to steal cement with which to build bunkers for hiding. The plan was to put the bunkers under the ghetto's stinking septic system to throw off the bloodhounds the Germans used to hunt Jews.

While sneaking back carrying a 100-pound bag of cement, he was shot in the leg by a German patrol. Leaving a bloody trail, he somehow got back.

But his father knew the Nazis would see the blood and look for him if he failed to show up at the next morning's roll call.

Another ghetto doctor came to him.

He had no instruments, but sterilized a coat hanger as best he could and dug out the bullet from Abraham's leg.

With his leg bandaged tightly to stop the bleeding, Bursztajn said, Abraham made it to roll call and helped build the bunker, which eventually hid—and saved—fifteen Jews.

Despite his complex history, Tom was, in some ways, a simple man. He loved the Shaker folk song "Tis a gift to be simple." He was also a Buddhist. In fact, it was his Buddhism that prompted us to take our most adventurous trip—to Burma, now Myanmar.

I confess I had a panic attack the whole time—for the

foreignness of it all, the dirt, the poverty, the military regime, and most of all, for the fact that, according to the terms of our group visa, we were not allowed to leave the country before our seven-day trip was over. Armed guards had met us at the airport. The only currency was cigarettes and whiskey. The women were so thin I could have almost encircled their waists with my two hands.

We couldn't understand a thing except for what our English-speaking guide told us. The Burmese alphabet, or what we saw of it on signs, was beautiful but incomprehensible. I could never get used to the ever-present soldiers.

Yet, I am so glad I went. In Rangoon (now Yangon), we visited an aging Associated Press journalist whom one of my *Globe* editors had met while covering the Vietnam War. The man was skinny, gracious, and effusively thankful for the sterile syringes, antibiotics, and other precious items we had brought for him. He mesmerized us with his stories of being imprisoned for writing antigovernment statements (which further fueled my passion for journalism). Later, I could sense the tangible power of Buddhism while walking in silence around the Shwedagon Pagoda. It was a feeling of wordless awe, a sense of community as Tom and I walked with other hushed people, round and round. No music, no sermons, no imposition of scripture, just breath, soft footsteps, the pagoda itself, and the sky.

Eventually, my travels with Tom began to dwindle when he was diagnosed with cancer—first, lymphoma, then several years later, with prostate cancer. His cancers were devastating, the first one more for me, the second, worse for him.

But there was one gift that helped both of us through some of the tough times, a friendship I had developed with a woman dying of breast cancer. I spent more than two years chronicling Nora's experience for a twelve-page special section of the *Globe* about hospice care. To this day, I have a large picture of Nora in my study. Her bravery in the face of death helped me confront Tom's impending death several years later. Her courage helped Tom more calmly anticipate his own.

Pain of Watching Nora Die

I never set out to become friends with Nora Lenihan. When we met in the spring of 1994, everybody—including Nora—thought she had about two months to live. I hoped to be sensitive and empathic, but I also expected to maintain a certain journalistic distance. And I confidently assured my editors that my story on her final weeks in hospice care would be ready by fall.

At first, I was so nervous around Nora that I could barely look her in the eye and say the word "death." After all, she was only thirty-eight years old, younger than I, and she was dying of breast cancer, a disease that I and most women dread. In fact, I found her situation so unbearably sad I wasn't sure I wanted to keep seeing her.

But Nora was so articulate, so honest, and so at ease talking about death that I soon found myself looking forward to our visits. Most of my twenty-three years in journalism had zoomed by in a blur of deadlines. This was obviously different.

It began to seem crass and ridiculous to rush back from Nora's Medford apartment to the *Globe* (though I did) to write some other story for the next day's paper when Nora's deadline—how literal that word became—was so much more cosmic.

Week by week, my visits began to be oases of calm, a chance to feel grounded in the ebb and flow of life and death, a time for talking about life's deepest feelings—mostly Nora's, but over time, mine as well.

I remember the day we became friends, as well as writer

and subject. I arrived as usual, making small talk as I got out my tape recorder. But I couldn't make myself turn it on. Suddenly, it seemed cruel and inhuman—as well as impossible—to pretend I was just a journalist with no feelings about what I was doing.

I cried, apologizing for what I felt was injecting my feelings into the process. I told Nora how sad I was that she was going to die, how I could barely tolerate that thought. I worried aloud about breaking the unwritten journalistic rules about getting too close to the people we write about.

And I told her about the pledge I had made to myself driving home from my first interview with her: that if it came to a choice between being a good human being to her and being a good journalist, I would choose the former.

She was touched and delighted. In fact, eight days before she died, she reiterated how pleased she was, not just that I was documenting what she called her "mission" to tell people about death and dying, but about our unexpected friendship.

"You took a risk to do something that wasn't easy," she said shortly before she died. Taking my hand, she told me she loved me and how pleased she was that she "got a deep friendship out of the deal. That was just icing on the cake."

Then, like some wise old editor, she added, "If it was going to be a really good story, I think that it required me to know you . . . I have very good thoughts about your willingness to do that for me."

I broke other journalistic rules as well. When I wrote the first draft of the story—18 months before Nora died—she asked to read it. There is a dictum in journalism that sources not see stories before they are printed. But I felt, and my editors agreed, that because Nora would not be able to see the story when it came out after her death, she should read it. And she did.

Michele McDonald, the photographer on this project, also got very close to Nora, often spending the night at Nora's when things were rough and, toward the end, helping to organize the schedule by which Nora's friends took turns caring for her.

As our story and these friendships evolved, Nora had dinner at Michele's house and at mine. She knitted clothes for the baby Michele and her husband were adopting from China. She came to several concerts of my singing group, the Back Bay Chorale. We exchanged small gifts at Christmas and on birthdays.

Nora threw a small birthday party for me four months before she died and, a month before her death, gave a baby shower for Michele. Today, Michele feels profoundly that "coming to know and love Nora changed me and changed my life." I do too.

Yet this came at a price.

As my commitment to Nora deepened, I found my visits with her were taking so much time that I couldn't see her during the week and still get my other work done. So I often saw her on weekends and kept in phone contact during the week.

The more involved I got, the more I had to juggle our friendship with my marriage and the needs of my parents, who lived two hours away and had begun to have medical problems of their own.

I also hated the uncertainty of never knowing whether Nora would be sick or well when I saw her, and never knowing when her death—and my grief—would come.

As Nora's journey in hospice unfolded, I felt increasingly

angry, not at her, but at our healthcare "system." The more Nora thrived, the more frustrated I felt that for too many Americans, the only way to get the kind of gentle, patient-centered care that Nora got was to be in hospice. "Why on Earth," I would fume as I drove home from her house, "does a person have to be dying to get that kind of respect and control in our modern, supposedly sophisticated medical system?"

As Nora's death approached, both Michele and I began spending more and more time with her, feeling deeply our commitment to be with her when she died.

Yet we were both almost unable to be there.

In mid-April, Michele and her husband went to China to pick up their baby. They had no control over the travel date assigned by the Chinese, and Michele was in agony, torn between her family-to-be and Nora.

Globe photographer Joanne Rathe stepped into the breach and took pictures in Michele's absence. But Nora had one ground rule we had vowed not to break: Only Michele would be allowed to take pictures of her death.

For two weeks, Michele and I kept in touch as best we could by fax and phone, and to everyone's enormous relief—including Nora's—Michele and the baby made it back in time.

Unexpectedly, I cut things even closer.

In early May, it became clear that Nora had just days to live. On the Sunday before she died, I visited her, then came home to find my telephone message light blinking. It was my mother calling to say my father had had a massive stroke.

Initially, we thought he would live and we planned to bring him home to my parents' house in Connecticut for hospice care.

By Wednesday, though, it was clear that, like Nora, my father had only days, perhaps hours, to live. I was completely torn. I felt I should be with my father, despite all that he had done to me and our family, but I wanted to be with Nora too.

I rushed down to Connecticut on Wednesday night, held his hand and told him I loved him. I also said, for the sake of the truth I had promised myself to acknowledge, that he and I had had our differences. I didn't elaborate. I didn't forgive him. After all, he never acknowledged any wrongdoing, and he was dying. He seemed to hear nothing, but I was proud of myself for speaking up, and for telling him I loved him.

I came back at midnight, calling Nora's sister en route.

On Thursday morning, my mother called to say that my father had just died and that the family would gather the next day at their home. Thursday afternoon, still shell-shocked, I went to see Nora, who was clearly in her last hours.

Exhausted, I went home. That night—actually, at 1:30 the next morning—Michele called. Nora had just died.

I rushed over for the last time to see and touch the woman who had become so dear to me and to grieve with the other women who had cared for her for so long.

As I try now to absorb these deaths that will be forever paired in my mind, I think of all that Nora taught me. About the profound uncertainties of life. About how human beings can keep on growing, even in the worst of times. About how people can sometimes find a courage that is astounding.

I feel unbelievably humbled by Nora's example. I hope that as my own life and challenges unfold, I can do half as well.

I didn't know it then, when I wrote those words for the *Globe*, but my challenges with Tom's health would soon intensify just as Nora's had. Ironically, soon after Tom learned that he had pros-tate cancer, on top of the lymphoma he already had, it was Nora who helped us gain a bit of perspective. We had gone to a birthday party at Nora's house, knowing it was probably her last such celebration. I whispered to her about Tom's latest medical news. "It's a bump in the road. Just a bump in the road," she told us, even as her own cancer was spreading relentlessly throughout her body. She took our hands and gently wished us well.

And when the time came for Tom to die, we coped. Together.

Tom and I spent months planning his memorial service.

Ever the control freak, Tom set out to manage things. Every Sunday, or so it seemed, he put me through his own unique version of what we called "death training." I hated it. He drilled me on how everything worked: finances, annuities, furnaces (upstairs and down), the persistent mystery of how to record TV shows, which lawyers to call for what, who the best plumbers were, on and on. There were always new topics to cover in my training, and I despised each and every one of them.

"But you're not dying," I protested. "We don't have to do this yet. Let's do something fun."

Something fun, at least by comparison, turned out to be planning his memorial service, a process eerily similar to planning our wedding.

We chose the music—Brahms's Requiem, to be sung by my singing group, the Back Bay Chorale. We chose which of Tom's lifelong friends would speak. We pored over poems and readings, taking turns getting teary-eyed. We settled on the venue—Harvard's Memorial Church. We recruited a minister friend to officiate.

Tears fell often onto my notes, dimpling the paper, smearing the ink. To compensate, we took frequent hugging breaks, standing together in our sweats and socks in our Sunday morning living room, just holding each other, no words needed. Or possible.

Tom, a scientist to the core, decided to donate his body to medical research, sort of like applying to grad school in reverse. He filled out the paperwork for Harvard and UMass, just in case. (Harvard, we discovered, can reject you even if you're dead if you have a disease they're not interested in.)

Tom mused about buying a gun in case his pain, like that of his father, who also died of prostate cancer, became unbearable. I argued for hospice and heavy drugs. Or, at the very least, no sudden, unilateral moves without telling me first.

Between worsening treatments—radiation, surgery to repair damage from the radiation, hormones that should have slowed the cancer but didn't—we managed some vacations, even slower-than-usual hiking trips. Eventually, he had to spend time in the chemotherapy room at MGH where brave dying men lay, stoic, poisons dripping futilely into their veins. Tom wouldn't let me go with him to that room. Too hard on me, he said; too hard on him to have me there, too.

As he worsened, the death planning took on more urgency. Where to put his ashes? I suggested Church Island on Squam Lake, near the family camp where we spent many happy summer weeks. He agreed. I added Mount Auburn Cemetery, so I could visit whenever I wanted. "Fine," he said, knowing this was more important to me than to him.

As death crept closer, Tom used his remaining energy to take care of me. From his bed, he managed the work crew he had hired to repair the roof, knowing I'd never remember to do it. He had the deck of the upstairs back porch redone, too, so I wouldn't be tempted to move downstairs.

"You wouldn't be safe downstairs as a woman alone," he said.

"I'd be closer to the garden," I protested.

"It's not safe."

In rapid succession came blocked kidneys, increasing pain, tubes everywhere, and me, the alleged nurse, clumsily changing dressings on his kidney tube incisions and irrigating his bladder. Finally, diapers; home health aides who didn't show; the awful day when the phone died, the repairman came, rang the bell, then disappeared; and the ambulance that, for reasons I never did learn, failed to arrive.

Let the More Loving One Be Me

At the very end, snuggled together in bed, Tom brought up the memorial service.

"There's another piece of music I want," he said quietly.

"What?" I snuggled closer.

"Ob-la-di, ob-la-da, life goes on. The Beatles song."

"Life goes on?" I asked, incredulous. How could life possibly go on? A solitary tear rolled down his face.

The memorial service went just as we planned—the tributes, the Brahms, the packed church, the funny stories at the lunch afterward.

After Tom died and had, one last time, gotten accepted into Harvard, where his body taught new med students about cancer and anatomy, Harvard sent his ashes to me. I parceled out the ashes into half a dozen plastic baggies to be sent to different relatives. The baggies were top of the line—the expensive kind with nice, easy-slide red zippers. I burst out laughing. Tom hated needlessly expensive things. I drove back to the store, bought cheap baggies with no zippers, and repackaged the ashes. I swear I could hear him laughing.

But that night, alone in the empty bed, "Ob-La-Di," the song he had chosen for his service, played over and over in my head.

"Ob-la-di, ob-la-da, life goes on . . ."

To my utter amazement, it did.

CHAPTER SEVEN

ᏳHealing

L ife did indeed go on, whether I wanted it to or not. Howie, a
newly widowed friend and the husband of a dear friend of mine,
and I formed an informal, two-person support group shortly after
our spouses died within a few months of each other. We decided to
meet every Sunday morning—otherwise, the loneliest time of the
week for me—for brunch.

"The world used to be in color," Howie said one day as we
ordered our pancakes at the S&S Restaurant in Cambridge. "Now
it's black and white."

How right he was. And so, we talked and talked and talked.
We shared feelings. Tears. Laughs. Memories. Dreams, especially
dreams, fascinating dreams. In our dreams, Laura spoke to Howie,
Tom spoke to me. As the months ticked by, the dreams began
to change, becoming less frequent, unconsciously processing our
grief for us.

I also devoured books on widowhood, which helped a bit. I
read and reread Joan Didion's wonderful book *The Year of Magical
Thinking*, which helped a lot. She wrote about her own experience with her husband's death. As she described her panic, I felt
less alone with mine. As she wrote of her sorrow, I softened into
mine.

I joined a bereavement group, too, which was also invaluable.

In one session, a woman walked in slowly, sat down in one of the easy chairs, tilted her head back against the headrest, closed her eyes, and remained mute for the entire session, a picture of utter grief and exhaustion. My grief, my exhaustion too.

I took some other positive steps. Eager to fill the house with life—young life, new life—I bought a purebred poodle puppy, promptly named Noodle. I bought a kitten, too, Lucky Lady. I joined a folk dancing group.

And I turned to the things that had always lifted my spirits and brought me joy, most importantly, singing.

There's something magical for me about singing, perhaps because it combines rigorous discipline with exuberant freedom. In fact, it's through the precision of tone and rhythm and pitch and blend that the freedom and expressiveness of music are created. It's the opposite of sloppiness. The more accurate I am with pitch and rhythm, the more my soul soars and my voice blends with everybody else's, sometimes miraculously generating perfect harmonic overtones, those ringing chords.

I do it all for fun, like the more than forty million other Americans who sing regularly in choruses. And it turns out that singing, especially choral singing, has a lovely side effect: It's demonstrably good for body and soul. It's as if evolution, in her wisdom, had given us an extra way to bond, and bonding has obvious survival value. Research suggests that singing with other people may raise levels of the feel-good hormone, endorphin. Singing in groups may even have helped early humans form larger cohesive groups than other primates.

Choral singing may be good for the brain and the immune system, too. In one study, scientists took samples of saliva before and after a rehearsal and a public performance by a professional chorus singing Beethoven's *Missa Solemnis*. Levels of a beneficial immune chemical increased significantly, while levels of the stress hormone cortisol declined. In less scientific terms, the singers said the performance felt like a "peak experience," with strong feelings of transcendence.

For me, it's those moments of musical transcendence, whether from tenderly singing lullabies to my newborn son or, later on, to my grandsons, or joining my voice with the voices of a hundred other people, that make singing so addictive for me.

Every Monday night from seven to ten, about a hundred of us gather in a big room in Emmanuel Church on Newbury Street in Boston: Young music majors with perfect pitch, aging folks with newly wobbly voices, doctors with silenced beepers, lawyers freed from briefcases, even the odd journalist glad to be where things are off the record. Technically, this is the Back Bay Chorale, an audition-only chorus. In truth, it is church, it is family, it is home.

There, lumped by voice part and melded by friendship, we cast off the masks we show the world, masks that scream, "Look at me! Look at me!" Here we became egoless, just a voice, one voice among many, striving, just for now, to not stand out—no unplanned solos, please—but simply to be part of every chord.

I confess that I once did have an unplanned solo moment. It was Christmas 2005. We were crammed together, elbow to elbow, black music folders almost touching, balanced on narrow risers at Boston University's Marsh Chapel, singing our hearts out to the festive, sold-out audience. We were just entering the gorgeous, pianissimo part of my favorite Bruckner motet, *Os Justi.*

Suddenly, my knees went watery. I swayed slightly into my friend D. D. next to me. My stomach lurched as a wave of nausea rose to the back of my throat. I stopped singing and started mouthing the words. Frantically, I wondered if I could hold on through the Bruckner until a more raucous carol came up, when I might be able to execute my escape by crawling out through the basses' legs to the back riser, sliding down, and slithering away backstage.

It was not to be. I swayed more, now forward and back, not just side to side. I tried with my eyes to signal Julian, our conductor, that something was wrong, not that I had any idea what he could do about it. I knew my face must be deathly white. But Julian was oblivious, blissed out by the Bruckner, as I had been until just moments earlier. "I'm not going to make it" was my last conscious thought.

Moments later, I woke up in the dead-silent church, lying amid scattered members of the chorale. Crashing forward, I had mown down the three rows of singers in front of me. The doctors in the group quickly mobilized. One asked if I had diabetes. I mumbled, "No." Another asked if I had a heart condition.

"No."

Julian called a brief intermission. Friends escorted me down to the basement where the restrooms were. I sat there, nauseous, in the cold hallway as the glorious music started up again upstairs. My worst nightmare—an inexplicable fear of fainting during a performance, a fear I had had for decades—had come true. Luckily, I haven't fainted again since, but my chorus friends still tease me every concert.

Despite this humiliating episode, which turned out to be the onset of the stomach flu, I still find it magic on Monday nights, this coming together to transform black notes on a page into soaring sound. It's still goose bumps and smiles every week, smiles that telegraph, "Wow! This is fun."

Whatever my mood at the beginning of rehearsal, I drive home singing—lighter, more connected. More at peace.

It wasn't just singing that helped calm my soul after Tom died. I began swimming regularly in pools most of the time, and in good weather, outdoors. I had been a good swimmer ever since my mother's early lessons and, thanks to her, had never been afraid of the water. But now I began to take swimming more seriously, in part for its considerable health benefits. Unlike jogging, swimming isn't too bad for joints, though shoulders can sometimes take a beating. Swimming is also a full body workout—arms, legs, core, glutes, back. It's aerobic, if you swim fast enough. And it burns calories.

But the more I swam, the more swimming became not just exercise, but a kind of moving meditation, not the exuberant connectedness of choral singing, but a kind of solitary tranquility, just gliding softly in a familiar yet somehow otherworldly environment—water.

There's a magic little pond—ironically called Great Pond—near the tip of Cape Cod. It lies hidden in the woods, a quarter of a mile or so down the pine needle path from the road. There's a rickety wood stairway down to a microscopic beach. Every once in a while, the town fixes the broken stairs.

You leave your sandals, towel, and car keys under a branch, grab your swim goggles and flippers, and step carefully down the splintery steps. You are alone; the pond is still as glass. It's late afternoon. You gasp slightly. The water is probably warm, but it feels cold around your ankles. You adjust your goggles, take a breath, and curl down into the water to slip your flippers on.

You look up and spot the first float, way over there, near the two Adirondack chairs where nobody ever sits. You know exactly where the weedy parts of the pond are, and the long, leg-entangling lily pads. If you forget where these slimy things grow, you find them the hard way when they snag your foot. You startle, gasp, back away fast.

By the deep part of the pond, you hit your rhythm: a gentle six-beat kick to match the easy rhythm of your arms. You're a waterborne metronome. You could go on forever. The water is soft, giving way soundlessly to your stroke. It's effortless, this carving softly through the water as each hand breaks the surface.

Too soon, you're at the next float. You reach up to hold the ladder for a minute, adjust your goggles, tipping out the water that has invaded. Then, back in again, counterclockwise around the pond. You always swim counterclockwise, though you don't know why.

Soon you're passing a dock beyond which you spot lawn chairs and kids' bikes. Strange. No noise there. Where is everybody? You keep going. In the distance you spot the farthest float down by the shallow, weedy cove. You tip your head up every few strokes to make sure you're heading straight for the float, then resume looking for fish underwater. There are none to be seen, only an old tire lying on the bottom, doing no harm.

Finally, at the float in the cove, you glance back toward the stairs you descended to enter the pond. Nobody there. Perfect. You head for one final float, where an older couple sometimes sits on chairs they have taken out to the float in their canoe. They are not there today. You hang on to that ladder for a minute, spotting your next target: a tall tree all by itself. You head for it.

You look down under the water again, arms and legs still strong. Finally. A big trout, followed by a smaller one. They swim together, away from you.

The home stretch. Still, nobody on the stairs. No kids splashing each other. No mothers chatting waist-deep near the shore. No fathers with little ones on their shoulders.

Just you. And the pond. Peace.

To my surprise, swimming eventually became a competitive sport for me, not just a way to get calm. I had never been a competitive athlete in my younger years, though I did have to survive a keen competition to become a cheerleader in high school. But despite cheerleading, field hockey, basketball, and softball, I had never had to compete directly against other athletes. And against the clock. A clock where not just seconds, but hundredths of seconds made the difference between victory and defeat. Indeed, the whole idea of competition initially felt like something women of my pre–Title Nine generation were not supposed to do.

How delightful it was, then, in my sixties, to learn how to compete—hard—against one of my dearest friends. And to celebrate together no matter who "won." And how delightful, in my sixties, to join the swimming organization US Masters, and to compete not just in regional but in national competitions and, once, in an international event in Italy. (I did well, backstroking my way into the middle of the pack of women in my age group.) Like swimming, competing on a team has yielded not only a stronger body but a whole group of new friends.

I crouched on the starting block; hands spread on either side of my left foot. My left toes, with their vibrant purple polish, were curled over the front edge of the block, my right foot firm against the back brace, head slightly up, eyes on the water.

The bleacher crowd chattered away, eating, glued to iPhones, not focused even slightly on the swim meet, the New England Regionals. My teammates, in their blue Cambridge Masters T-shirts, were busy too, sipping Gatorade, nibbling brownies, and obsessively checking and rechecking heat and seed times.

"Swimmers take your mark!" the starter's voice boomed through the loudspeaker.

I raised my body into a track start, shifted more weight to my front leg, energized my back leg, leaned forward. Seven women on the other blocks did the same, including my dear friend Alice.

Wait. Wait. Wait.

"Go!"

I reacted fast as the other women flew off their blocks, too.

I dove into the water hands first, head tucked. I dolphin-kicked hard. I felt strong, young, undulating from chest to toes, hands outstretched, eyes on the black line on the bottom of the pool. Hard, hard, this was the fastest part of the race, underwater, not breaking streamline to surface and breathe. Five, six kicks. Finally, I tilted my arms toward the surface, flutter-kicking now, eyes up. It was light up here. Air. Good.

I broke the surface, hands together, then pulled back hard with my right arm, rolling onto my left side, pushing water back hard toward my right hip, then rotated toward my right side, pulling hard now with my left arm, right arm out, reaching forward for the next "catch." Right hand bent downward, got it, pulled hard, hard. Again. Again. The plastic lane marker slipped by.

I was almost at the wall. One last pull with my right arm, I dove head down, somersaulted. I flipped my turn, toes stabbing the wall. On my back now, I rolled to my left, then onto my stomach. Good. I surfaced, breathed, pulled, kicked. Through my peripheral vision, I could see the colorful finish line flags overhead. It was only a 50, thank God. Just fifty yards.

Bring it home! Bring it home! My silent chant. I could see no one, hear nothing. No breathing once I got inside the flags. Just pull, kick. I slammed hand-first into the underwater electronic time board.

Done! Did it! I twisted around to see the scoreboard high on the wall. "Foreman, J, 40:21." Whoopie! I beat the qualifying time for Nationals, 41.79.

Then, shock. Shit. Two years ago, I did these same fifty yards in 37.14, about three seconds faster. My best was getting worse.

Another shock: Alice beat me. To be honest, she always beats me in freestyle. That's okay—she's five years younger, so it doesn't count. She's in a different age group. Psyche rebalanced, friendship intact, I hoped for tomorrow. Backstroke, my best event. My last chance this year to prove to myself that I'm not getting older.

Backstroke day came. Alice and I studied the heat sheets. To our collective dismay, we were in side-by-side lanes.

"Don't show me up," she said, worried, unzipping her orange fleece jacket and unwrapping the towel from around her waist. I always beat her in backstroke.

"No chance, sweetie pie. You'll do great."

"Your kick is so strong."

"So's yours."

We jumped into the water for the backstroke start, feet on the timing pad, hands gripping the gutter.

Healing

"Swimmers, take your mark!"

I pulled up with my arms, knees tucked to chest. Focused.

"Go!"

I arched backward, deep. My backstroke start is a killer. I can dolphin, sleek, on my back for fifteen yards.

Shit! I was not dolphin-kicking, I was doing a flutter-kick. I was barely moving. I never mess this up. What happened? I switched to dolphin, rattled, pissed. I surfaced early, crooked, hit the lane line.

Think!

I approached the wall, turned fast onto my stomach, flipped my turn. Better now. I pulled hard, kicked like crazy. Pull. Kick. Strokes sloppy but strong. Eternity. Finally, the finish line flags. I pulled again, once, twice, kick. Glide.

I reached backward. Where was the wall? Time stopped. Where was that wall? I had practiced this so many times, but today, I stopped stroking too soon. Losing momentum, I glided, so s-l-o-w-l-y, finally touching the wall. I twisted to see the scoreboard.

45.19. Fast enough to qualify for Nationals by more than six seconds. Again! I won my age group. (Not that it was much of an age group. The only other swimmer got second.)

Alice had out-touched me again, by less than a second. Okay, she's still younger.

But that was not the point. I'd lost again to my younger self. Two years ago, I did 42.85, about two seconds faster.

In the shower, Alice and I hugged, laughed, congratulated, commiserated.

"Sweetie pie, I'm two seconds slower than I used to be. I can't believe it."

"I am too," Alice said. "All my times are three or four seconds slower than last year."

"That makes me feel better."

We gathered up shampoo, conditioner, towels, and hit the locker room, peeling out of our tech suits.

"We're old. But at least we're still swimming, you know? How many people our age do that?"

"Yeah. That counts," she agreed. "Savino's tomorrow night? Wine and tapas?"

"Absolutely."

One of the best things about swimming in a pool, of course, is that there are no sharks. Or seals. Or huge waves. Or kayakers, motorboats, sailboats, ferries. There is also a nice black line on the bottom of the pool to guide you along and lane lines to keep you from straying.

So why, not once, but twice, did I sign up for a crazy harbor swim event in Provincetown? It wasn't the chance to contribute to efforts to combat the AIDS epidemic, although that played a part. And it wasn't just a chance to do another competitive event. I had already done a number of sprint distance triathlons, which involve an approximately half mile swim in the ocean, a 12.5-mile bike ride, and a 3.1 mile (5K) run. I still can't answer that "why?" question. But it sure was fun.

"I'm old-ish," I said to the earnest young woman at the check-in desk, whispering my age to her as I put my canvas tote bag down, the sleeves of my wet suit flopping over the top, my goggles threatening to jump out before it was too late. I fished in my purse for my pen.

"Wow!" She glanced up, a "that's really old" expression flashing across her otherwise polite face.

"I know," I said, anxiety creeping up another notch. "I'm old. Too old to be doing this."

"No, no, it's great." She recovered gracefully. "I wish my grand-mother would do something like this."

I am a grandmother, I thought. I'm twice as old as most of these people here.

"Here" was Provincetown, the grayish morning of the annual

Healing

haphazardly organized AIDS benefit involving a 1.4-mile sprint across Provincetown Harbor from Long Point Light to the beach near where I was now having my race number written in black magic marker on my bathing cap and on my arm, in case, I presumed, I washed up cold, dead, and otherwise unaccounted for—a DNF, or Did Not Finish—later today.

The harbor had been beautiful yesterday, calm, blue, sailboats bobbing at their moorings, not a shark fin or even a seal in sight. Today, however, the waves looked like they were four or five feet high, dotted by whitecaps. Far in the distance, much farther away than it usually looked over the rim of a martini glass from Ross's Grill, a P'town restaurant and bar, lay Long Point Light.

There were about five hundred of us, some silently studying their gear, some chattering excitedly, all of us wrestling to get our wet suits on, joking that this was the hard part. And in a sense, it was. Wet suits do not like to be occupied—they don't mind a leg or two, but they fight being pulled up over hips and bellies (not to mention other female protuberances higher up), they balk at arms being pushed down sleeves, and resist to the death being zipped up the back.

In groups of twenty or thirty, we were ferried by Flyer's shuttles for the fifteen-minute boat ride out to Long Point.

We shivered, clustered together on the sand near the lapping waves. The big, strong guys and some women claimed the front row spots; the rest of us scattered messily behind them. When the start whistle sounded, we rushed, hundreds of us, into the water.

No sooner had I begun to get horizontal and started to swim when an aggressive guy knocked my goggles off. By accident, I'm sure, but I sputtered and muttered a few choice oaths.

I chugged along, gradually separating from the masses, content to be in the middle of the pack. Every few strokes, I had to stop and tread water for a second or two to spot the Provincetown water tower, which was in the sight line to the beach that was our destination. I watched some swimmers head off in the wrong direction toward Wood End Light, setting themselves up for an unnecessarily long swim; I watched others veer to my right, heading for Truro, another costly deviation. Bothersome as it was to keep stopping to see the water tower, this kept me on a relatively straight course.

The waves, though, were miserable, not least when, over the crest of a wave coming at me from the right, a kayaker, who was supposed to be one of the lifeguards, shot down the wave and smacked me in the head. More curses.

And then, at last, I was in the harbor, swimming around the moored sailboats, the beach finally in sight. I made landfall in just under an hour. Though shivering violently, I was ecstatic.

Now, many years later, I still look out to Long Point Light, then glance at the harbor. I allow myself a well-deserved moment of pride: I swam that.

CHAPTER EIGHT

ᏩFinding Love, Yet Again

While swimming and singing steadied me and helped me learn to slowly take in the stubborn fact that Tom was never coming back, what helped the most in my post-Tom life was little short of a miracle.

A happy confluence of job shifts prompted my son and his wife to decide to move with their three-year-old son and brand-new baby from New Mexico to my house in Cambridge. Suddenly, my house was really alive again, not just me and the cat and the dog, but people. My people. I was not alone anymore.

We certainly respected each other's privacy. But I could hear them coming home. I could see their car parked near mine. We could share a pizza and ice cream. I could babysit. And one day, my older grandson gave me the best compliment I have ever had.

We were standing on the front porch, ready to get in the car. I was taking him and his friend, the boy next door, for an outing in Boston. The kids were excited, practically dancing with delight.

My grandson suddenly looked up to say goodbye to his parents and sang out, "We're going to the science museum. With Grandma Judy and *no grown-ups!*" I still smile when I remember that.

Let the More Loving One Be Me

After a year or so, with my domestic life settling into security, I screwed up my courage and decided to take the plunge. Again. I took off my wedding ring and set about dating with a fury. I was determined. I'd loved being married—the coziness of it all, the snuggling, the quiet times, watching TV on the couch, dinners together. I wanted to do it again. After all, I was only sixty-three. Even with my young family around, I didn't want to be single for the rest of my life.

Initially, I dated some losers, and Tom, as always, quickly set me straight. In a dream, he told me firmly, "Stop dating jerks."

I did, and began aiming higher. My friend Howie asked me what kind of man I was looking for.

"A musical doctor," I said unhesitatingly. I knew the medical world well from all my years as a medical writer and health columnist at the *Globe*. And I had been a singer all my life. Dating became my part-time job. I was serious. I wanted a partner.

I signed up for as many dating services as I could find— eHarmony, Lunch Dates, Match.com.

Ah, yes, Match.com.

"Serious guy looking for serious fun," read his entry on Match.com. He was a physician, his essay said, sixty-seven, and into mind-body medicine. He had been married for thirty years and had grown children the age of my son. He lived nearby. His picture was blurry, but he looked benign, fit, and down-to-earth.

Most importantly, he had written to me first! A live one! This time, I wouldn't have to send my fragile heart out into cyberspace, only to be met, once again, with silence. Or worse, tattoos and motorcycles.

He had been drawn, he wrote in his email, to my essay, which began, "I was happily married for twenty-two years, and I want to do it again." I was sixty-three and had no wish to get stuck with a guy who couldn't commit, who might leave me dangling halfway between movie dates and marriage.

Finding Love, Yet Again

Bingo! It was love—at least for me—at first email.

I was a plunger-in-er. He was much more cautious. But after a few tentative phone conversations, and before we actually met, I finally screwed up my courage. He had a Jewish last name. My last name was ambiguous.

"There's one possible deal-breaker here," I told him on the phone. "I'm not Jewish, and I'm guessing that you are. Is that okay?"

"It's fine," he said. I did a spontaneous little jig in the kitchen. "My first wife wasn't Jewish either."

And so, we met at the Bristol. A serious restaurant. He really was serious. I was, too. I spent $70 to get my hair done . . . for a first date.

I got there early and sat on a small sofa in the corner, where I could watch people. Coattails flying, a man rushed up to the "maître d." A big bounce in his step, he radiated confidence, energy, and athleticism. And he had hair! Beautiful, neatly trimmed, salt-and-pepper hair that was, at least in places, longer than mine.

After the first round of wine and appetizers, he told me his story. His Match.com blurb had said only that he was a physician, though he was actually a shrink, very interested in mind-body stuff, Buddhism, and meditation. (Made in heaven, I thought.)

Yet, for all that, he wasn't pompous or stuffy. His face, a contrast of deep creases, yet smooth skin, and sparkling eyes told its own story. He told of the pain of his divorce. (A man who can talk about his feelings! Joy!)

My heart was open, and he could tell. He took my hand, right there at the table, in his own warm, competent one and squeezed. I melted. His warmth filled me. He was so there, so present, so with me.

I stroked his hand. His nails so neatly trimmed, the muscles in his forearm begging to be touched. I think we danced between dinner and dessert. I'm not sure. I may have sung "The Girl from Ipanema" in Portuguese at the microphone with the Brazilian band.

We stumbled outside into the Public Garden. The night, though late October, was only slightly chilly. He held my hand. How long had it been since someone did that? I shivered. He put his arm around my waist. I leaned in. He was so solid, so warm, so male.

The trees looked cozy in the dark, the park benches alluring. We sat, bodies touching now. We looked at each other. Yes, it was okay to kiss on the first date. Wasn't it? We were in our sixties. Why not?

And did we kiss—long, sweet, tender. My God, he was so warm, so sexy. Without planning it, we were soon in each other's arms. His hands stroking my back underneath my jacket, on top of my blouse. (Dimly, I struggled to maintain some sense of propriety. "Not on the first date," some voice said. My mother's? What was she doing here?)

Reluctantly, we stood up, walked, body pressed to body, back to the valet parking. My car came out first. I left him standing there waiting for his, looking as dazed as a thirteen-year-old on a first date.

I think this guy will call me, I mused, laughing as I drove away. He did.

That very night.

In a very real way, I have Tom to thank for Ken. In little things, like grocery bills and restaurants, Tom was such a skinflint that people teased him about it mercilessly, even at his memorial service. But in the big things, like leaving me the house in his will and setting up an annuity plan for me, he was generous to a fault. And no more so than in love. He wanted to make sure I would not be lonely after he was gone and gave me the most precious gift one spouse could give another: his blessing to find love again.

Here in the Swiss Alps, high above the little town of Zermatt, the snow was sparkling, the air crisp. It was cold at this altitude—seven thousand feet—but here, unlike in dreary Boston, the cold felt invigorating, cheery even.

Hiking uphill, we had stripped down to just a few layers—no gloves, no hats, no neck gaiters. We'd stuffed our outer jackets into our backpacks.

Finding Love, Yet Again

Ken, my husband, a physician who had loved Switzerland ever since he went to medical school in Zurich fifty years ago, was behind me on the trail, hiking strongly like the athlete he still was. He was seventy-four now, the age that Tom had been when he died nine years ago.

My hiking boots, laced up snugly, pounded a steady squeak with each step, my trekking poles reinforcing the rhythm. Left foot, right pole, right foot, left pole. It was effortless, this rhythm, my breathing automatically synched to my steps, my mind free to soar on its own.

"Vinn-ter, Vaaan-der, Vaaay-gen, Vinn-ter, Vaan-der, Vaaay-gen," I chanted silently. It was German. "Winter Wanderwegen" meant "winter hiking trails." The vowels stretched out on their own to match my steps. I was in the zone.

Subtly, beneath my consciousness, my silent song shifted. Now, my feet were marching to an older, different rhythm. "Jungfrau, Monch, und Eiger, Jungfrau, Monch, und Eiger," this time, too, the vowels stretched out with "eyeeee-ger" just long enough to fit my steps, the same steps I had taken all those years ago in these mountains with Tom.

Tom and I had spent many summers in these Alps, where the three big mountains—Jungfrau, Monch, and Eiger—towered above us, hike after hike. Tom was a strong hiker but often lived in his head, even amid this magnificent scenery. Born in Vienna, he remained fluent in German all his life.

To get Tom, a laser physicist whose mind often wandered to abstract things, back to the present, I would stop on the trail and ask, "How do you say in German, 'Look at the view, Tom. You've paid for it.'?" He would smile self-consciously at the money reference: "Shau die Natur an, Thomas, du hast fur Sie bezalt." We'd laugh, and he'd be "with me" again in the mountains, at least for a while.

Even back in Cambridge, he always felt somewhat the foreigner, despite having lived in the States since he was eight or nine years old. Driving around, he would spot a police car.

"Polizei, polizei," he would say.

"They won't hurt us, Tom. We're not doing anything wrong." But, of course, the Jews hadn't been doing anything wrong either.

After the first cancer, and then the second, we still hiked, more slowly but with no less enthusiasm. When traveling became impossible, we walked around Fresh Pond, or to Harvard Square and back. By that point, Tom was pale, and he was drinking more coffee than he used to in a vain effort to recover the energy he had lost to his cancers and their treatments.

Toward the end—I hadn't realized how close the end was—I quit working to take care of him. He was sleeping most days and nights in a separate bed. I was relieved. I dreaded the idea of waking up with him beside me, dead.

The night before he died, I lay down next to him. He was not conscious anymore, but he was still alive. "I love you, Tomshi," I said, using my favorite nickname for him, the one his mother used to use. A tear rolled silently down his face. He heard me.

After he died, I opened a letter he had written to me a year earlier. At that point, neither of us, of course, could have known how long he had, and he wanted to be sure to record his thoughts while he still could.

In it, he told me how much he loved me and gave me his blessing to remarry if I had the chance. That blessing was the greatest gift I ever had, the most generous of presents—the love of one good man encouraging me to find another.

"Stay to the right," I heard the resonant voice behind me as we came to an open place where the hiking trail crossed a ski run. "Watch out for the skiers."

Ken's voice brought me out of my reverie. Oh, that voice, that baritone.

On my seventieth birthday, Ken used his voice and delighted me by getting out his guitar (untouched for years) and gustily, sweetly singing, "You Are My Sunshine" to me and our assorted birthday dinner guests. He hunted a bit for chords but finally let it rip, bringing down the house.

Finding Love, Yet Again

When he sang in the car on our way to the Cape, I melted. He was never more himself than when he sang—his spirit, his joy, his enthusiasm for life. His whole body would get into it; he would dance in his seat while he drove. At home on the NordicTrack, he would put on the same old Creedence Clearwater CD every night and pump away, belting out the songs—between gasps for air—at full volume.

Today, as always, Ken was so very present, this living gift that Tom's generosity had allowed. Different as they seemed on the surface—Tom was a quiet introvert; Ken, a voluble extrovert—these two men would have liked each other. Both Jewish—but both more Buddhist in their thoughts and meditation practices—they are similarly caring, though Ken, perhaps because he was a shrink, understood me better than anyone ever has.

So now, after lunch in the sunny restaurant watching the skiers, we reluctantly headed down the trail again. By now it was midafternoon, but the sun was still strong, the Matterhorn still rising majestically in front of us, Zermatt still far enough below us to give us plenty of time to get back before dark.

We walked along in silence, accompanied only by the sound of our boots and poles squeaking in the snow, our two rhythms now one.

"Ken."

He stopped on the trail to face me.

"A line from a poem just popped into my head. I think it's by W. H. Auden."

"What is it?"

"'If equal affection cannot be, let the more loving one be me.'"

We looked at each other, stunned by the wisdom of these few words. Our eyes filled with tears.

"That's like a marital vow," he said, gathering me in his arms.

"It is," I answered. "Let the more loving one be me."

"No," he said, burying his head in my neck. "Let the more loving one be me."

⌒

Ken was not just a gift in himself, but as a psychiatrist, too, he changed my life profoundly. He introduced me to a type of therapy he had begun using with his own patients, one I had never heard of: Internal Family Systems or IFS, a type of therapy developed in the 1980s by psychologist Richard C. Schwartz.

I was skeptical. By the time I met Ken, I had already had tons of therapy, starting when my marriage to Bruce, my first husband, broke up.

My first therapist was, in reality, a kind, gentle, older man, completely unlike my father. Yet in talking to him, I learned how much I was projecting my fear of men and authority figures onto him. Slowly, dimly, I began to realize how deeply fearful I was of my father, and of men in general.

With my next therapist—a wonderful, caring woman—the therapy went a bit deeper. I vividly remember one session in which we literally knelt on the floor together while she held my hand and I spoke aloud to a pillow representing my father about how terrified I was.

It wasn't so much a fear of him per se—after all, "he" was just a pillow. What I began to realize was that I was terrified of *feeling the fear itself*. I truly believed that if I allowed myself to feel that fear that I would literally die. Such was the power of the taboo my mother had instilled in me about *feeling* my feelings.

My therapist after that was another wonderful woman who practiced CBT, cognitive behavioral therapy. I learned with her how to identify the harmful thoughts that were triggering my anxieties and to distance myself somewhat from them. I learned some thought-stopping tricks. If I caught myself thinking, "I'm a mess today," I learned to stop and think, "Don't go down that path." Initially, I'd have to tell myself not to continue down that path multiple times a minute, then multiple times an hour.

To my amazement, my mood would improve over the course of that day.

But none of this therapy was as powerful for me as the IFS that Ken introduced me to, which in my case meant Beth, a gifted therapist who sat with me hour after hour, week after week, year after year until I was finally able to sit by myself with the parts of me that had held so much terror and sadness all my life.

IFS therapy is a bit like the idea expressed by the thirteenth-century Persian poet Rumi, who wrote:

"This being human is a guest house. Every morning is a new arrival. A joy, a depression, a meanness, some momentary awareness comes as an unexpected visitor ... Welcome and entertain them all. Treat each guest honorably. The dark thought, the shame, the malice, meet them at the door laughing, and invite them in. Be grateful for whoever comes, because each has been sent as a guide from beyond."

IFS is based on a similar idea—that within each of us, there are different "parts," different "selves," different subpersonalities, each with its own feelings and beliefs. The mind, in other words, is like a family in which the members have different levels of maturity, wisdom, pain, and reactivity.

In IFS therapy, you learn to identify and name these different parts, to "talk" to them out loud or in your imagination, to understand each part's feelings and where those feelings came from, and ultimately to allow your mature, centered self to run the show and create peace among the parts because you have truly "heard" and understood their stories.

Writer Elizabeth Gilbert, author of *Eat Pray Love* and other books, is a well-known devotee of IFS therapy. She writes of a situation with a toxic friend. "Part of me felt victimized and self-pitying, part of me felt like I was being oversensitive and should just shake it off, and part of me was so fierce that I dreamed of taking the bastard's head off."

She goes on to name three of her most prominent parts: Lizzy, an anxious little kid who lives in terror of conflict and abandonment; Elizabeth, the inner creator who's artistic and a writer; and Ms. Gilbert, her most "grown-up" self, who brings peace to all the parts.

Psychiatrist Dr. Bessel van der Kolk, also a fan of IFS and author of the best seller *The Body Keeps the Score*, describes a recent encounter with his parts: "Right now a part of me feels like taking a nap; another part of me wants to keep writing. Still feeling injured by an offensive email message, a part of me wants to hit 'reply' on a stinging put-down, while a different part of me wants to shrug it off."

In the IFS model, the goal, with the help of an IFS therapist (believe me, it's hard to do it on your own), is to learn to identify your different parts and heal the wounded ones with the help of your centered, adult self.

In Schwartz's model, parts usually fall into one of three major categories. One category is the exiles, what Freud would have called repressed feelings. The exiles, as the name implies, are parts of us that have been unconsciously cast out, disowned, buried deeply so that we can survive and go on with the rest of life. Exiles often carry psychological trauma, as in my case, the sexual abuse of my father and the deep sadness from my mother's emotional neglect. When I first became more aware of my exiles, I hated them. I didn't want them to be part of me, to be part of who I was. It took ages to feel compassion for them.

Exiling feelings is a kind of unconscious coping strategy. As van der Kolk puts it, "Coping takes its toll. For many children, it is safer to hate themselves than to risk their relationship with their caregivers by expressing anger or by running away . . . If you are abused as a child, you are likely to have a childlike part living inside you that is frozen in time, still holding fast to this kind of self-loathing and denial."

A second category of parts consists of the protectors, which come in two forms—the managers and the firefighters. The managers run our day-to-day lives and try to keep control of every situation so that the exiles stay hidden. I love my managers—the competent reporter, the energetic athlete, the responsible friend.

The firefighters are really desperate protectors who will do almost anything to keep the exiles from breaking through and demanding attention. Firefighters can be alcohol, drugs, violence, even extreme overwork—anything to shove the frightening feelings back into the murky depths.

IFS therapy involves slowly "unburdening" the exiles, gradually learning that it is safe *not* to carry around so much fear or sadness or anger. One of my exiles, for instance, which I visualize as a cute toddler, is a little child who loves to play and sing and listen to stories like any normal kid, but who also carries around the weight of my mother's rejection.

So my task in the therapy has been to let go, not of the little kid herself, but of the burden she had been carrying, the heavy sack of sad, scared feelings. It's amazing how real this process is. When I allowed myself to feel the genuine sadness my little exile was carrying, I literally felt lighter.

Ken and I have used IFS as couples therapy too. I've learned to recognize that sometimes, when he's angry, it's really his hurt little exile coming to the fore. He's learned that when I'm anxious, it's often my little exile feeling abandoned. Together, we've learned that when we argue or fight, it's usually our respective protectors that are bumping into each other. The more we've understood this marital back-and-forth, the faster we figure out why we're clashing. And the closer we've become.

But it's not just therapy that has led to more moments of serenity, it's the growing recognition, as I age, of the impermanence of life itself. Impermanence, for me, is simultaneously the most relaxing and the most terrifying of thoughts.

It was May 2016. Sally, my dearest friend since freshman year in college, had just learned she had a recurrence of lung cancer. Her world, and mine, changed in an instant.

Three years earlier, Sally had nursed her identical twin, Patty, through her final days with lung cancer. They were so similar it was spooky. They were both classmates of mine at Wellesley. They got identical scores on the SATs and thought they had even missed the same questions. Their tumors were almost identical too. Patty's was diagnosed first. Sally, out of an abundance of caution, had gone to get checked out. Bad news. She had cancer too. Neither had ever smoked.

It's funny—well, not very—how different everything looks the minute you or someone close to you gets a terrible diagnosis. Gone in a flash are the unconscious assumptions—that life will continue indefinitely as it always has, with the usual ups and downs, dinners, work, movies, kids, friends. That's what normal is, right? The certainty, or its illusion, which is just as good, that there are no disasters threatening, no surprises hiding in the wings. Just the expectable, the routine, the everyday things you count on without thinking.

Then, all of a sudden, comes the realization that all this has changed, that this new, horrible knowledge, once known, can't be un-known, can't be banished. Even if you try to make it disappear, it shows up in your dreams or your nightmares.

The first time my world went from happy to terrified in a matter of seconds was when Tom got lymphoma. We had been married only five years and I was still relaxing into the delicious delusion that I had finally found my safe haven, a place where love and work were simmering along in harmony.

When we first heard the diagnosis, Tom, then sixty-three, was philosophical, figuring he had dodged a lot of bullets until this point and was long overdue for trouble. I, on the other hand, did not feel overdue for trouble. I had had enough growing up. I was devastated. That first night home, Tom wanted to make plum jelly. I wanted to talk and cry. He set about making an Indian dinner. I raged at him for pretending everything was normal.

"Why not make plum jelly?" he said. "Why not have pleasure?"

"Because I can't."

The lymphoma never left my mind, though I think it left his from time to time. He was good at distraction. I wasn't. A good friend whose husband had died of lymphoma warned me that cancer never leaves your consciousness.

"You never forget about it, ever," she said. She was right.

I could never forgive myself for being the upset one. Here was Tom, the one with cancer, all calm and controlled. I was the one falling apart.

"You have the tougher job," this kind husband kept saying to me. "You will have to go on without me. I won't have to go through that."

"But you'll have to die," I cried.

"That's true," he said, squeezing me tight. "Can we read our books now?"

With the second cancer, prostate, our roles switched, at least somewhat. He was scared because he had watched his father die, castrated and bedridden, in severe pain from this same horrible prostate cancer.

Strangely, the more upset Tom allowed himself to be, the easier it became for me. I could be the strong one, the caretaker, and I was. The more the crises bunched up, the more trips we made to the purgatory that is Mass General's emergency room, the more I finally had something to do. I was still devastated. But at least I was useful.

When Tom did die—a remarkable eleven years after the first diagnosis—I grieved mightily, heart and soul. And yet, after a year or so of deep sadness and yearning, I began to lose that unreal sense of living in a parallel universe, a universe where things looked normal but weren't.

It was wonderful, being back in the real universe. It was a new normal, of course, and a lonely, frightening one. But there was nothing hanging over my head. That sense of impending doom left me when Tom finally died. Doom had happened, and I had survived.

Then came Sally's diagnosis, and after that, the recurrence. Once again, I was in that parallel universe. Sally and I, collectively, had had four much-discussed marriages. We had been each other's chief cheerleaders through blossoming careers, taking genuine pride in each other's accomplishments. We had collectively raised three kids, with frequent phone consults. I was the godmother of her kids. So many dinners and sails and hikes. So many talks.

There was something different this time, though, and not just because Sally was my best friend, not my spouse. Tom had been twelve years older than me. We knew when we married that he would probably die before me. Which meant that my death, even as his approached, would probably be far away.

Sally and I were the same age, within a few months. We were classmates. This time, my own mortality stared at me when I looked at her. This time, our time on earth felt finite. Letting this reality sink in, not fighting it, was the new challenge.

Sally and I lived that challenge together. We kept up our lunches and our phone chats, only the conversation became more about chemo regimens, clinical trials, immunotherapy. We pored over scientific papers together, deciphering the odds of long-term survival, which were never good. When, on top of everything else, Sally broke her foot, we obsessed together over the pros and cons of surgery for an immunocompromised person. Too risky, she decided wisely. So, she limped around in a cast for months. Through it all, she kept working as major anthropology awards began pouring in. Her colleagues were increasingly concerned as well.

Our friendship deepened by the week as her disease progressed and further still when the talk inevitably turned to hospice. My visits became more frequent. Despite the raging COVID pandemic, I sat by her bed week after week, my mask securely on and my fingers crossed.

A few days before she died, we held each other's hands and looked deep into eyes that we knew so well by now. We told each other how much this fifty-eight-year friendship meant to us both, and how we would hold one another dear forever. We said goodbye—me, in tears, Sally, not quite.

And then, like Tom, Sally was gone. That parallel universe was parallel no more. This was the real universe after all. Death, life, all of it.

Buddhists have long embraced the concept of impermanence. I am still new to it. If the center of the parallel universe is fear, the core of the real universe is acceptance of impermanence.

I am not there yet. But I am beginning to catch on. Perhaps there is just one universe after all, the impermanent one. The only one we have.

CHAPTER NINE

Impermanence

The years with Ken have flown by, mostly very good years, with some wonderful trips to Switzerland, England, the Caribbean, and especially—the trip of a lifetime—a photographic safari in Botswana and South Africa.

Though in our seventies by then, we were both in good health and eager for adventure. We bounced for days in Toyota Land Cruisers with other good-natured souls from all over the world. Grandparents taking kids along as graduation treats. Singles hoping to meet each other as well as animals. The guides were spectacular, able to spot a cheetah that we could barely find with binoculars, spotting the remains of a snake-on-wild-dog attack just by looking at the squiggles in the dirt.

There were times when, in our little cabins in the game parks, we were in actual danger—from wandering elephants, lions, snakes, and God knows what else. Armed guards had to escort us to our rooms after dinner every night. Out in the park during the day, we were not allowed out of the jeeps except for brief, well-guarded pit stops.

But for all that actual danger, I had never before felt such a sense of peace. We've had similar moments of peace, too, sitting on the deck of the house we bought on Cape Cod, watching the sun set over the distant water.

Let the More Loving One Be Me

But these sweet moments have been punctuated with pain, health scares, and health challenges too. These realities, once unthinkable, have stealthily crept into our lives. On the plus side, the first of these, a horrible battle with chronic pain, led me to write two nonfiction books.

I never knew such pain existed.

My neck suddenly went haywire—a long-lurking arthritic problem exacerbated by too many hours hunched over a new laptop. On a subjective scale of zero to ten (there is no simple objective test for pain), even the slightest wrong move—turning my head too fast or picking up a pen from the floor—would send my pain zooming from a zero to a gasping ten.

Sitting in a restaurant was agony—if the table was too high, it forced my arms and shoulders up, making my neck tense. Sitting at the movies looking up to see the screen was agony, too. Shifting from sitting or kneeling on the bed to lying down was excruciating—there is no way to avoid that transitional moment when nothing supports the weight of the head. Even little things like bending forward to paint my toenails became impossible.

During these episodes, which happened many times a day for months, I couldn't talk through the pain, though mere words couldn't have captured the pain's intensity anyway. So new, shocking, and incomprehensible was all this that I felt utterly alone, convinced that no one had ever felt like this before.

That, of course, was not true. I discovered that a hundred million other American adults suffer with chronic pain, though this is largely a silent, invisible epidemic. People with chronic pain don't make headlines, though they do kill themselves twice as often as other people.

I tried to cope by myself, with handfuls of ibuprofen, lots of stretching, and extra computer breaks. I kept working, hosting my weekly radio talk show, going to the gym, swimming three times a week. I kept singing and performing with my chorale. (And, of course, I kept hanging out with friends and family. Best of all, I continued to enjoy time with Ken.)

But as the months ticked by, and the pain only got worse, I sought help from the medical system, a system I thought I knew well, having covered it for decades. As the *Globe*'s "Health Sense" columnist, I probably had the best address book in town, filled with the names of hundreds of eminent doctors.

But a funny thing happens when you become a powerless patient, not an on-top-of-things journalist. The medical system I encountered as a person with pain was shockingly different from the one I thought I knew. It was almost completely unprepared to help.

My first doctor, a pretty, young physiatrist (rehabilitation specialist) who came highly recommended, was initially nice. But over the course of our visits and escalating medications and injections, she grew angry when I didn't get better. At one point, she told me, coldly, that we had ten minutes, during which we could either talk or I could get "trigger point" injections. During what would end up being our last visit, she seemed to imply that my pain was caused by some emotional problem. I wanted to scream, "You bet I'm emotional. I'm in agony."

Eventually, an MRI (magnetic resonance imaging scan) showed several almost-herniated discs in my cervical spine, as well as vertebrae sliding over each other (a condition called spondylolisthesis) and bone spurs stabbing my nerves. My facet joints (small joints that help stabilize the spine) showed arthritic damage.

In essence, my inflamed, irritated cervical nerves were firing almost nonstop, causing the trapezius muscle in my left shoulder and neck to spasm. The spasms in turn caused my head to twist bizarrely to the left (a condition called cervical dystonia), where it would stay "frozen" for long periods, forcing me to use both hands to turn my head back to a more or less normal position. The resulting pain was twofold: A searing, burning nerve pain that ran in a straight line from my neck to the top of my left shoulder, as if acid were dripping right onto the nerve. And severe muscle spasms.

Let the More Loving One Be Me

After eight months of no progress—despite temporarily giving up work, swimming, the radio show and singing—I finally began to get better when I saw a team of doctors who believed me. They did not suggest the pain was all in my head. They knew I was not exaggerating. They gave me time, kindness, respect, cortisone shots, and very rigorous physical therapy called "boot camp."

I was grateful, of course, but sobered. It had taken eight doctors, multiple physical therapists, an acupuncturist, several massage therapists, an ergonomic consultant (who got me to buy all new office furniture), and drugs, including opioids, before I began to get better. Ultimately, it was exercise and physical therapy that fixed me.

When my pain finally improved enough so I could work again, I wrote a column for the *Globe* detailing my journey through pain and my frustrations with the medical establishment. The response overwhelmed me. Patients called to thank me and to tell me their stories, many of which were far worse than mine. An ear, nose and throat doctor called to tell me he had almost committed suicide because of unrelenting pain. Scientists called to beg me to write about their new discoveries in the underlying mechanisms of pain.

There's a book here, I thought. I started reading, visiting scientists in their labs, and listening to patients. I discovered that in terms of sheer numbers, chronic pain is a bigger health problem than cancer, heart disease, and diabetes combined. I found that it is absurdly expensive—costing hundreds of billions of dollars a year. And I realized that almost nobody cared.

So, I wrote a book on pain, and then another, in paperback. Reviewers—bless them—praised it. Patients cried in gratitude. Sales were good.

And nothing has changed.

I became a voice for people in pain. But I was still a voice crying in the wilderness.

And then came a health scare I will never forget.

Impermanence

November 4, 2021, 10:15 a.m.

Mammogram day. I arrive at one of Boston's most esteemed hospitals, early and anxious. I'm always anxious before my annual mammogram, and this year, I'm edgier than usual because I haven't touched base in advance with my dear friend, Bonnie. Bonnie knows absolutely nothing about medicine, but for decades she has been my magic charm for mammogram anxiety. It'll be fine, she always tells me. And I've always tried to believe her.

The mammogram hurts today, as always. How could it not, with each breast getting smashed between two slabs of hard plastic. But who cares? It's the results I care about. In the old days, my wonderful radiologist did my mammograms and read them right away. He'd give me the good news, then we'd chat for a few minutes and I'd be on my way. Another year of freedom. Another bullet dodged.

This time, I have to wait. The day after my regular screening mammogram, the nightmare begins, quietly. I learn through the patient portal system that I have to go back for diagnostic imaging of the "questionable calcifications" on the left, and possible "architectural distortion" on the right. There is a number to call.

I call right away. I cannot have the second mammogram and ultrasound, I'm told, until December 13, five weeks away! The system, not a friendly doctor as I'd once had, has just told me that I might have cancer or even two different kinds of cancers, one in each breast, but I won't find out for at least five weeks because this hospital is "fully booked."

Fully booked? I can't believe this wait can be blamed totally on COVID-19. I suspect pre-existing, patient-unfriendly hospital bureaucracy as well.

Waiting for anything can be agonizing. For a loved one to call. For a college acceptance. For a needed paycheck. Stressful, but normal. Waiting for medical test results? Excruciating. And, to my mind, at least somewhat avoidable.

Granted, growing cells in culture or analyzing pathology specimens takes time. But when "the system" chugs along at its own sluggish pace, when doctors or their surrogates don't call back promptly, when online patient portals give only partial information? That's unforgivable. And would be fixable if patients, not bureaucracy, always came first.

The basic dictum of medicine is *primum non nocere*: First, do no harm. But being made to wait for weeks to find out if you have cancer, or any other serious disease for that matter, is harm. It evokes fear of the unknown. The oldest and strongest emotion of mankind is fear, and the oldest and strongest kind of fear is fear of the unknown, as horror writer H. P. Lovecraft put it. Philosopher and writer Joseph Campbell interpreted the struggle with what he called our greatest fear this way: Many of us would enter a tiger's lair before we would enter a dark cave.

As humans, we crave information to help us understand everything that comes at us every day. What underlies the fear of the unknown is the perceived absence of information at any level of consciousness, wrote psychologist R. Nicholas Carleton, who has studied the phenomenon, in a 2016 paper. And unpredictability makes it worse. In experimental settings, people show more stress if there is a 50 percent chance of receiving an electric shock than if there is a 100 percent chance, according to a 2016 study published in Nature Communications journal.

On the surface, this does not make rational sense. We should be only half as anxious if there's only half the risk. But that's not how our minds work. With uncertainty, the brain—particularly the fear center, the amygdala—revs up into a state of hypervigilance.

And so, I wait. I meditate. I swim. I do my relaxation tape. I swim some more, two miles at a time. I use a meditation app on my phone. I wait.

Some days, I can concentrate on work. Other days, I'm imagining a double mastectomy, reconstruction, Stage 4 cancer. I google madly, pore over reliable websites, print out reams of cancer data. And I fume. Cancer wasn't in my life's plan. It's not in anybody's. I'm stunned by my own anger. Why would I expect to be any luckier than anybody else?

Impermanence

And I'm angry at the hospital that did the mammography. Couldn't the mammography center predict how many questionable scans like mine are likely on any given day, then plan to save slots the following day for subsequent tests?

I call my primary care physician who, God bless her, works the system and gets me in for the second round of mammograms sooner, just a week away.

November 11, 2:45 p.m.

Breast imaging at a different top Boston hospital.

Two gentle radiologists do more mammography and ultrasound. "We have to do some sampling," says the senior radiologist. "I'm afraid I have to use a scary word, 'mass,' on the right." The left seemed less worrisome.

I lose it. "You mean I could have two different cancers?" At least I can ask the doctor in front of me right away.

"It's possible," she says.

I ask for Ken. He comes in, strokes my back. Double biopsies are scheduled, eighteen days away. We go out to eat. I have a martini and a half. He does too. The fear is running away with me.

I go home and log onto the hospital's online patient portal. I need more information. I click on the little envelope icon that suggests I might be able to initiate contact with the radiologist whose name appears on the test results. No luck. She's not listed as one of my available contacts.

I try calling. No luck. The hospital switchboard has no record of anyone by this name. I ask about the other radiologist, but she also seems to be unknown to the hospital. I persist. I learn that she's gotten married and uses a different last name now, not yet updated in the system. When we finally connect by phone, she repeats the results I already have but doesn't elaborate on them to me. That's for another doctor to do.

I wait some more. I meditate. I'm up to two-and-a-half-mile swimming sessions now.

Let the More Loving One Be Me

November 29, 10:15 a.m.

Biopsy day. Finally.

Again, two radiologists. They patiently describe the biopsy procedure to me, step-by-step, then narrate the procedure as they continue their work. The lab tech stands where I can see her and chats kindly with me throughout. Thanks to lidocaine, the procedures are almost painless. Loaded up with ice packs and care instructions, my husband and I leave, get home, and crash. We sleep for two hours. We know it will be three to five days before we get the results. Compared with the past month, that feels bearable.

December 1

As I drive home from an errand, one of the radiologists calls. I pull over, get out a pencil and paper.

The left side is benign. The right, she tells me, has "invasive tubular" cancer.

I've never heard of tubular cancer and, googling later in the day, learn that it's rare and not too bad. I am remarkably calm, so happy to know. Knowing even something awful is so much easier than not knowing. I'm free of that horrid anxiety, the prison of fear.

The minute I get home, I tell Ken, then swing into action. I email some doctors I'd been lucky to meet over decades of medical reporting for the *Globe*, asking for help. What's invasive tubular cancer? How bad is it? Am I going to die? They email right back, cutting short the weeks it could've taken to get the information they give me if I hadn't been a reporter.

One oncologist source is especially reassuring. This is the most nothing of all breast cancers, he tells me, with zero chance of threatening your life. I know I still have to have surgery and nobody has told me yet who's in charge. A surgeon? I have no idea whom to call now. Still, I'm delirious.

I'm also curious about the hormone receptor status of my cancer, knowing from all my years of reporting that many breast cancers feed on estrogen or progesterone or both, and that will affect my treatment plan. Back to the patient portal. My test results file says information on hormone status will be forthcoming as an addendum. No addendum follows. I email my primary care doctor again. She gets the results and tells me: The cancer is positive for both hormones. Why the patient portal can tell me I have cancer but not tell me the hormone receptor status is a mystery. Hospital bureaucracy again?

Then, suddenly, I'm in the system at the Dana-Farber Cancer Institute, a place I've written about for decades. I never thought I'd be a patient there.

Now, phone calls are returned quickly. Appointments are set up efficiently. Nurses call with questions. A COVID test is set up. I'm no longer lost in medical limbo, unable to get information, unable to figure out who's in charge.

I'm optimistic. A plan is in place. I have surgery to take out what's left of the mass. I can no longer take my beloved estrogen. I will have hot flashes. But I'm alive. It'll be OK.

And the next time my mammogram rolls around, I'm calling Bonnie beforehand.

As I write this now, I hear Ken playing the piano. He, too, has had some bad news. So far, the meds have worked their magic. But individually and together, we speak more these days of impermanence. We still hope for many more years together, many more sunsets, maybe another trip, more time with grandkids—his and mine. We know that this life we have cannot last forever. But at this very moment, we are more in love than we've ever been. Our "protectors" still clash now and then. We still have cars to get inspected, condo bills to pay, weight to lose. But we are grateful. Very, very grateful.

Sometimes, when I'm alone, thinking about the people I have loved who have died, a poem by two Jewish rabbis comes to mind.

Let the More Loving One Be Me

It starts like this.

"In the rising of the sun and in its going down, we remember them.

"In the blowing of the wind and in the chill of winter, we remember them."

It goes on for several verses. I whisper the lines to myself, my throat tightening, until it ends ". . . so long as we live, we remember them." Oh, I do, I do. I will, I will.

Other times, when I'm sitting in my fold-up beach chair at sunset, staring at a placid ocean, feeling a slight breeze, the words of the poet Mary Oliver bring tears to my eyes.

"To live in this world, you must be able to do three things: to love what is mortal, to hold it against your bones knowing your own life depends on it; and, when the time comes to let it go, to let it go."

But how? How is this possible?

I think of Tom's choice of Beatles music for his memorial.

"Ob-la-di, ob-la-da,

Life goes on . . ." It does. But how?

I am not wise, like the people who wrote these words.

I'm not the Buddha who, I imagine, could contemplate the idea of impermanence peacefully.

I'm not like my swimming friend, Wendy, still fighting pancreatic cancer for all she's worth, yet saying, "It's not so bad once you get comfortable with the idea of death."

She is. I'm not. Once in a while, I get glimpses of being comfortable about my own death. Sort of. Not really. What I can't stand is the idea of Ken dying, or my son and his wife, or my grandkids.

I'm not a saint, or even a great meditator. I'm just a regular old human, lucky in some ways, not so lucky in others, doing my best, being nice, mostly, being content, being sad sometimes, trying to understand what we're all doing here.

"I don't want anything to happen to you." I cry on Ken's shoulder.

"Something will happen to me," he says gently. "Something will happen to you too. How do you think I would feel if you weren't here?"

Impermanence

"Terrible," I say, knowing it's true. He nods.

There is a built-in grief to love. Even forever love is not forever, no matter how hard we try.

And that is what makes love so precious. I have few regrets in my life. Never learning to play the piano. Never taking physics. Not discovering therapy earlier.

But I do not regret a single moment of love, for people who have died and those, thankfully, still with me.

When Ken and I look into each other's eyes and hold each other, I know with utter certainty that his love for me, and mine for him, is all that matters. One day, his side of the bed, or mine, will be empty.

But in the rising of the sun, I will remember him. In the blowing of the wind, he will remember me.

CReferences

Chapter One

CDC. "Sexual Violence Is Preventable." Accessed January 29, 2023. https://www.cdc.gov/injury/features/sexual-violence/index.html.

The Center for Family Justice. "Statistics." Accessed January 29, 2023. https://centerforfamilyjustice.org/community-education/statistics/.

Finkelhor, David, Anne Shattuck, Heather A. Turner, Sherry L. Hamby. "The lifetime prevalence of child sexual abuse and sexual assault assessed in late adolescence," *Journal of Child and Adolescent Health* 55, no. 3 (2014): 329–33. https://pubmed.ncbi.nlm.nih.gov/24582321.

Masho, Saba W., Rebecca K. Odor, Tilahun Adera. "Sexual Assault in Virginia: A population-based study," *Women's Health Issues* 15, no. 4 (2005): 157–66. https://pubmed.ncbi.nlm.nih.gov/16051106/.

National Intimate Partner & Sexual Violence Survey. "Executive Summary." Accessed January 29, 2023. https://www.cdc.gov/violenceprevention/pdf/NISVS_Executive_Summary-a.pdf.

NSVRC (National Sexual Violence Resource Center). "Statistics." Accessed January 29, 2023. https://www.nsvrc.org/statistics.

RAINN, the Rape, Abuse & Incest National Network. "Statistics." Accessed January 29, 2023. https://www.rainn.org/statistics.

US Department of Justice, Office of Justice Programs. "Child Abuse." Accessed January 29, 2023. https://www.ojp.gov/feature/child-abuse/overview.

Chapter Two

Adult Children of Alcoholics/Dysfunctional Families. "Welcome." Accessed January 30, 2023. https://adultchildren.org.

American Academy of Child & Adolescent Psychiatry. "Alcohol Use in Families." Updated May 2019. https://www.aacap.org/AACAP /Families_and_Youth/Facts_for_Families/FFF-Guide/Children-Of-Alcoholics-017.aspx.

Bansal, Manjari and Neha Kashyap. "Adult Children of Alcoholics: 6 Vital Questions." January 27, 2021. https://www.webmd.com /connect-to-care/addiction-treatment-recovery/adult-children -alcoholics.

Black, Claudia. *It Will Never Happen to Me*. New York: Ballantine, 1981.

Esser, Marissa B., Sarra L. Hedden, Dafna Kanny, Robert D. Brewer, Joseph C. Gfroerer, and Timothy S. Naimi. "Prevalence of Alcohol Dependence among US Adult Drinkers, 2009–2011." *Preventing Chronic Disease* 11 (November 20, 2014): E206. https:// pubmed.ncbi.nlm.nih.gov/25412029/.

Mosel, Stacy. "What Are the Effects of an Alcoholic Father on Children?" American Addiction Centers. Updated September 15, 2022. https://americanaddictioncenters.org/alcoholism-treatment /alcoholic-father.

National Institute of Alcohol Abuse and Alcoholism. "Alcohol Use in the United States." Accessed January 30, 2023. https:// www.niaaa.nih.gov/publications/brochures-and-fact-sheets/ alcohol-facts-and-statistics.

Reinberg, Steven. "Many People Who Drink a Lot Aren't Alcoholics: CDC." November 20, 2014. https://www.webmd.com/mental -health/addiction/news/20141120/many-people-who-drink-a -lot-arent-alcoholics-cdc#1.

Yasgur, Batya Swift. "Adult Children of Alcoholics: Healing Lifelong Scars." May 30, 2017. https://www.psychiatryadvisor.com /home/topics/addiction/adult-children-of-alcoholics-healing -lifelong-scars/.

References

Chapter Three

Cozolino, L. *The Neuroscience of Psychotherapy: Healing the Social Brain*. New York: W.W. Norton & Co., 2010.

Kenley, Holli. *Daughters Betrayed by Their Mothers*. Ann Arbor, MI: Loving Healing Press, 2018.

Streep, Peg. *Daughter Detox: Recovering from an Unloving Mother and Reclaiming Your Life*. New York: Île d'Espoir, 2017.

Wallin, D.J. *Attachment in Psychotherapy*. New York: The Guilford Press, 2007.

Chapter Seven

Beck, R.J., T.C. Cesario, A. Yousefi, and H. Enamoto. "Choral Singing, Performance Perception, and Immune System Changes in Salivary Immunoglobin A and Cortisol," *Music Perception* 18, no. 1 (2000): 87–106. https://psycnet.apa.org/doi/10.2307/40285902.

Stewart, Nick Alan Joseph and Adam Jonathan Lonsdale. "It's Better Together: The Psychological Benefits of Singing in a Choir," *Psychology of Music* 44, no. 6 (July 7, 2016). https://doi.org/10.1177%2F0305735615624976.

Weinstein, Daniel, J. Launay, E. Pearce, Robin I.M. Dunbar, and L. Stewart. "Singing and Social Bonding: Changes in Connectivity and Pain Threshold as a Function of Group Size," *Evolution and Human Behavior* 37, no. 2 (March 1, 2016): 152–158. https://doi.org/10.1016/J.EVOLHUMBEHAV.2015.10.002.

Acknowledgments

I'm enormously grateful for all the friendship and support from my writer buddies at the Harvard Institute for Learning in Retirement.

About the Author

Judy Foreman is a former *Boston Globe* health columnist and the author of three works of nonfiction from Oxford University Press. In 2022, she published her first novel, *CRISPR'd*, from Skyhorse Publishing. A Wellesley College grad (Phi Beta Kappa), she spent three years as a Peace Corps Volunteer in Brazil and has a master's from the Harvard Graduate School of Education. She was a Lecturer on Medicine at Harvard Medical School, a Fellow in Medical Ethics, also at Harvard Medical School, a Knight Science Fellow at MIT, and a Senior Fellow at the Schuster Institute for Investigative Journalism at Brandeis University. She has won more than fifty journalism awards, including a George Foster Peabody Award and a Science in Society award from the National Association of Science Writers. She lives outside of Boston with her husband.

SELECTED TITLES FROM SHE WRITES PRESS

She Writes Press is an independent publishing company
founded to serve women writers everywhere.
Visit us at www.shewritespress.com.

The Girl in the Red Boots: Making Peace with My Mother by Judith Ruskay Rabinor, PhD. $16.95, 978-1-64742-040-6. After confronting a childhood trauma that had resonated throughout her life, psychologist Dr. Judy Rabinor, an eating disorder expert, converted her pain into a gift and became a wounded healer—a journey that taught her it's never too late to let go of hurts and disappointments and develop compassion for yourself, and even for your mother.

The Sergeant's Daughter: A Memoir by Teressa Shelton. $16.95, 978-1-63152-721-0. Every night of her childhood life, Teressa's sergeant father brings his military life home, meeting each of his daughters' infractions with extreme punishment for them all. At first cowed by her father's abuse and desperate to believe that maybe, one day, things will change, Teressa ultimately grows into a young woman who understands that if she wants a better life, she'll have to build it for herself—so she does.

Baffled by Love: Stories of the Lasting Impact of Childhood Trauma Inflicted by Loved Ones by Laurie Kahn. $16.95, 978-1-63152-226-0. For three decades, Laurie Kahn has treated clients who were abused as children—people who were injured by someone who professed to love them. Here, she shares stories from her own rocky childhood along with those of her clients, weaving a textured tale of the all-too-human search for the "good kind of love."

Letting Go into Perfect Love: Discovering the Extraordinary After Abuse by Gwendolyn M. Plano. $16.95, 978-1-938314-74-2. After staying in an abusive marriage for twenty-five years, Gwen Plano finally broke free—and started down the long road toward healing.

Now I Can See The Moon: A Story of a Social Panic, False Memories, and a Life Cut Short by Alice Tallmadge. $16.95, 978-1-63152-330-4. A first-person account from inside the bizarre and life-shattering social panic over child sex abuse that swept through the US in the 1980s—and affected Alice Tallmadge's family in a personal, devastating way.

Say It Out Loud: Revealing and Healing the Scars of Sexual Abuse by Roberta Dolan. $16.95, 978-1-938314-99-5. An in-depth guide to healing the wounds caused by sexual abuse, written by a survivor who's lived the process firsthand.